## THE COUNCIL OF CHIEF STATE SCHOOL OFFICERS

The Council of Chief State School Officers (CCSSO) is a nonpartisan, nationwide, nonprofit organization of public officials who head departments of elementary and secondary education in the states, the District of Columbia, the Department of Defense Education Activity, and five U.S. extra-state jurisdictions. CCSSO provides leadership, advocacy, and technical assistance on major educational issues. The Council seeks member consensus on major educational issues and expresses their views to civic and professional organizations, federal agencies, Congress, and the public.

## THE ASSOCIATION OF TEST PUBLISHERS

The Association of Test Publishers (ATP) is a nonprofit trade association for the international testing community, representing companies involved in developing and marketing assessments used in educational, organizational, clinical, and certification/licensure settings. ATP engages in federal and state advocacy efforts on behalf of the industry and provides educational activities for its members and users of assessments, including in the areas of professional development, intellectual property protection, test security, and emerging technology surrounding all forms of delivery, both paper and pencil and online.

COUNCIL OF CHIEF STATE SCHOOL OFFICERS
Mitchell Chester (Massachusetts), President
Christopher Minnick, Executive Director

Council of Chief State School Officers
One Massachusetts Avenue, NW, Suite 700
Washington, DC 20001-1431
Phone (202) 336-7000
Fax (202) 408-8072
www.ccsso.org

ASSOCIATION OF TEST PUBLISHERS
William G. Harris, Ph.D., Chief Executive Officer
Alan J. Thiemann, Counsel

601 Pennsylvania Avenue, NW
South Building, Suite 900
Washington, DC 20004
Phone (866) 240-7909
Fax (717) 755-8962
www.testpublishers.org

TECHNICAL EDITOR
James E. Carlson, Ph.D.
Educational Testing Service

# TABLE OF CONTENTS

# INTRODUCTION TO OPERATIONAL BEST PRACTICES

## Operational Best Practices for Statewide Large-Scale Assessment Programs

Following nearly four years of work, in June 2010, the Association of Test Publishers (ATP) and the Council of Chief State School Officers (CCSSO) jointly published the *Operational Best Practices for Statewide Large-Scale Assessment Programs* (*Operational Best Practices*). The 2010 Version has been widely acclaimed by stakeholders and has been used for various purposes, especially training, by the testing community and by state departments of education. The *Operational Best Practices* have become recognized as the seminal resource guiding operational decisions about statewide assessment programs, used as a complementary document alongside the long-standing scientific professional technical standards informing assessments, the *Standards for Educational and Psychological Testing* (*Joint Standards*), developed and sponsored jointly by the American Educational Research Association, the American Psychological Association, and the National Council on Measurement in Education. In fact, a recent report by the Government Accountability Office surveying state test security practices was based on the 2010 Edition of the *Operational Best Practices*. "K-12 Education: States' Test Security Policies and Procedures Varied," GAO – 13- 495R (May 16, 2013).

However, the ATP and the CCSSO, as the sponsoring organizations (Sponsors), recognized that state assessment programs are dynamic, especially with the advent of the U.S. Department of Education's Race to the Top initiative and specific funding of two national assessment consortia, the Smarter Balanced Assessment Consortium and the Partnership for Assessment of Readiness for College and Careers. During the development of the original document, the ATP and the CCSSO made the decision that the emergence of testing via computer would require expansion of that initial edition ("the 2010 edition") to cover topics related to assessments delivered and/or administered using technology. Moreover, with Race to the Top Assessments likely coming into use as early as the 2014-15 school year, the need to address technology-based assessments was seen as even more pronounced.

Accordingly, the ATP and the CCSSO announced when they released the 2010 Version of the *Operational Best Practices* that they would quickly commence a new effort to update the document, in order to address technology-related issues affecting large-scale state assessments. Indeed, the Sponsors established a website to collect comments and feedback from users. The organizations have availed themselves of this input as work commenced on updating and modifying the 2010 edition.

By early 2011, the ATP and the CCSSO had selected a new Working Group for developing the 2013 edition. The Sponsors wish to recognize Lisa Ehrlich of Measured Progress, Pat Roschewski, formerly of the Nebraska Department of Education, and Christopher Hanczrik of the Washington State Office of Superintendent of Public Instruction, who served as Co-Chairs, for their commitment and leadership on this project. The Sponsors also acknowledge the following members of the Working Group who devoted their time and energy to this project:

- Colleen Anderson, Iowa DOE
- Wes Bruce, Indiana DOE
- Suzette Stone Busa, The College Board
- Diana Cano, Educational Testing Service
- Jennifer Dean, Riverside Publishing
- Vincent Dean, Michigan DOE
- Antonia Deoudes, CTB/McGraw-Hill
- Nikki Eatchel, Questar Assessment
- Karen Squires Foelsch, Pearson
- David Foster, Kryterion and Caveon Test Security
- John Jesse, Utah DOE
- Ho Lee, CTB/McGraw-Hill
- David Mott, Tests for Higher Standards
- Bob Olsen, CCSSO
- Pat Roschewski, Data Recognition Corporation
- Sarah Susbury, Virginia DOE
- Alan Thiemann, ATP
- Debbie Willis, American Printing House for the Blind

Finally, the Sponsors are indebted to James Carlson of ETS, who served as editor for this project, bringing his expertise to the tasks of reviewing and analyzing the initial draft of the edition, as well as comments received during both the internal and external comment periods, leading to the final published product. The Sponsors also appreciate the efforts of Amy Brown of Measured Progress, who handled the administrative support and document management throughout the draft document development cycle.

This 2013 version of the *Operational Best Practices* is dedicated to Daniel J. Eignor, editor of the 2010 edition, as well as editor of the upcoming edition of the *Joint Standards*, whose life-long achievements in assessment, including these prominent documents, will be recognized by future generations of measurement experts and educators. The Sponsors proudly honor Dan and are grateful that he provided his insights and expertise on the first version of this project.

## Background

Some of the background presented in the 2010 edition provides a useful backdrop to understanding the context of this revised and updated *Operational Best Practices*. However, this information has been updated to provide a clear perspective on the process used in developing the 2013 edition.

In June 2006, the Association of Test Publishers (ATP) and the Council of Chief State School Officers (CCSSO) began discussions to identify and publish a set of voluntary, nonregulatory best practices for states and testing companies to use to strengthen implementation of statewide testing programs in the United States conducted under the No Child Left Behind Act (NCLB).

The original idea for developing a best practices guide actually came from the U.S. Department of Education, reflecting the belief that such a document would facilitate quality testing practices for the benefit of everyone affected by state testing programs, including schools, parents, and students. Regardless of future legislative changes to the Elementary and Secondary Education Act (ESEA), states and testing companies will always find advantages from understanding what procedures help to form quality testing practices.

In December 2006, the ATP and its testing company members agreed to form a working group (WG) to review sample documents and create a template for writing best practices that would be clear and useful to testing companies and states. Over the next eight months, the WG met numerous times and produced preliminary materials. CCSSO received periodic reports about this work, including a presentation at the Education Information Management Advisory Consortium (EIMAC) meeting in October 2007. Before the end of 2007, CCSSO agreed that state representatives would join the WG and commence joint work to draft a formal document. Since January 2008, the expanded WG worked diligently to develop the first edition and has continued that effort in developing the 2013 edition of the *Operational Best Practices*, which covers all major components of operating a large-scale assessment program, from procurement to reporting test scores. The topics covered by the *Operational Best Practices* are central to the tasks of designing, developing, administering, and scoring state assessments, and reporting state assessment results. Moreover, the operating practices described are considered to be reasonable and feasible, each having been reviewed carefully by both state assessment leaders and testing industry veterans who are very familiar with the complexities of specific functions of state testing programs (e.g., program management, shipping of materials, test administration).

Beginning in early 2011, the new WG began its work by first conducting a "gap analysis" of the 2010 edition, identifying chapters and topics where attention to technology-based assessments, either alone or in combination with paper-based assessments, would require additional and/or different practices. As much as possible, the new WG decided to retain existing substance and language of the document so that users who have already implemented practices based on the 2010 edition would not experience difficulties locating content or using the 2013 edition. However, the magnitude of changes identified in the gap analysis has required some adjustments and modifications to existing language, including some instances where substantive revisions have been necessary, or where it has been necessary to reorder materials and chapters. Where new material has been added, the WG has tried not to revise the 2010 edition language unless it was necessary to provide clarity or consistency.

The results of the gap analysis were sometimes significant in terms of the scope of the changes the WG concluded should be made. The most impactful set of changes involved additions to many chapters to set forth practices related to technology-based assessments (see subsequent discussion for definition and scope of this term) in a comprehensive manner that is parallel to those practices included in the 2010 edition for paper-based assessments. This change covered many areas, from program management, to item development and banking, to delivery, to administration, to scoring and reporting. But other topics related to the use of technology-based assessments also had to be expanded or modified: new problems in program design, new practices for test security, and the need to handle test accommodations for special populations. Indeed, as the WG contemplated how to deal with the challenges and complexities of accommodations, it decided to do so through the concept of accessibility for all students. Another change related to technology was the realization that many statewide assessment programs would not be all paper-based or all technology-based – so the concept of dealing with "mixed mode" assessment systems was chosen to capture these issues. Further, the focus on technology meant that there would be a need for the components of technology systems (e.g., hardware, software, communications networks) and assessment programs to be interoperable with one another (e.g., for the smooth exchange of data and content), so a new chapter on interoperability was developed. Finally, the WG determined that a state would benefit from having a "program design" chapter; consequently, the WG has included a pre-chapter entitled, "State Considerations for Assessment Program Design," to provide a basic checklist for a state to follow before it even prepares an RFP to select a service provider. Although the principle user of this checklist will be the states, service providers will also find this material instructive to gain an understanding about how states will go about the process of evaluating and modifying their current assessment programs when state laws change or when the assessment consortia activities come online.

As discussed above, the 2013 edition WG identified a threshold issue about how to characterize assessments taken by computer. Such assessments often have been characterized as "online;" however, today's technology results in the use of many assessments which are not paper-based but are not administered "online" with direct access to the Internet. In order to ensure consistency in articulating what best practices impact statewide assessment programs employing technology, the WG adopted a common definition (see below). Another element this discussion identified was that technology is moving so rapidly that it makes no sense to describe the delivery or administration of technology-based assessments in terms of devices that are currently available (e.g., desk top computer or other "Net-centric" device possessing computer capability, including hand-held, tablet, cellular telephone, or other type of personal digital assistant device). Consequently, the WG decided that the term "technology-based assessment" would be defined without reference to any specific device, platform, network, or system. Technology-based assessment is a term intended to replace prior references to computerized delivery methods (e.g., computer-based testing, online testing).

"Technology-based assessments" are administered by computer, in either stand-alone or networked configuration, or delivered by some other technology device that is linked to the Internet or World Wide Web, where the student accesses a digitally formatted (non-paper-based) assessment directly, or remotely through a local server that caches the assessment, or stores the assessment on some other medium (e.g., CD, USB flash drive), which enables its access without immediate direct access to the Internet. Unlike traditional paper-based tests, the student experience with technology-based assessments may vary widely. Technology-based assessments may be categorized by the purpose of the test (which may involve high- or low-stakes decisions about students), the types of responses required, the test design (e.g., adaptive), the testing environment (e.g., school computer lab, home), and the type of device used (e.g., laptop, desktop, tablet, smart phone).

As indicated in the 2010 edition, the scope of the *Operational Best Practices* is limited to large-scale state assessment programs; therefore, the Sponsors continue to acknowledge that this document may not be precisely applicable to different testing protocols and systems, including those used on an international basis. Nevertheless, the ATP and the CCSSO believe that this document provides a solid framework from which others might seek to define a set of practices tailored to their testing programs; accordingly, the ATP and the CCSSO encourage others to use this document for that purpose. Specifically, the Sponsors note the increased level of attention by districts and schools to many areas of testing quality (especially security); although this document is not directly written for local education agencies (LEAs), it provides significant and useful information to guide district and school personnel in the conduct of the state or local assessment programs.

Finally, the two organizations fully recognize that the testing process is dynamic; therefore, they expect that the *Operational Best Practices* will be reviewed on a periodic basis, updated to account for changes in technology or testing methodologies (e.g., a growing reliance on technology-based testing), to ensure that content remains viable.

## Continued Topics

This Introduction also covers the following topics that remain largely intact from the 2010 Version, with updates only to cover events since the original publication and modest changes in language:

• Sponsorship
• Criteria for Best Practices
• Review, Public Comments, and Final Adoption
• Use of the Document
• Terminology Used in the Document

## Sponsorship

This project is jointly sponsored by the ATP, representing nearly all testing companies that currently provide services to state assessment programs, and the CCSSO, including representatives of state departments of education or its state assessment directors group. Representatives of each organization participated fully in the development and review of the document. Going forward, publication and maintenance of these *Operational Best Practices* will be undertaken by both the ATP and the CCSSO.

## Criteria for Best Practices

In identifying and developing these *Operational Best Practices*, the WG applied several criteria to help ensure that the document describes proven practices that would provide concrete benefits to users. Each best practice had to:

- be directly related to the goal of enhancing operational test program quality, without conflicting with areas or principles specifically covered by scientific, professional technical standards embodied in the *Joint Standards* (see page 2);
- have a record of use by more than one state and/or testing company;
- be ready and available to be implemented by any testing company or state, without requiring, favoring, or advancing any particular technology choices to the detriment of others;
- be presented in a way that would permit alternative methods of attaining the same goal or objective; and
- be capable of being described through a measure related to its achievement or performance, rather than through specific requirements or prescribed steps or actions.

Only practices for which all participants agreed on their effectiveness were included. However, a consensus process was used for adoption of the substance and description of each practice.

## Review, Public Comments, and Final Adoption

From the outset of the development of the 2013 edition, as with the 2010 edition, the WG communicated with the testing industry and the states via written reports and presentations, including those at the ATP Annual Innovations in Assessment Conference, the EIMAC Conference, and the National Conference on Student Assessment.

Internal reviews of the draft of the 2013 edition *Operational Best Practices* were conducted for a period of 45 days within ATP and CCSSO, as well as by multiple testing company and state assessment staffs. The internal reviewers all had extensive experience with the various operational elements of designing and administering large-scale testing programs. Use of an online management tool, developed and managed by CCSSO, facilitated the gathering of internal reviews and allowed the WG to deal with a number of comments in refining the document into its final draft form. Final reviews of comments were managed by the Technical Editor, ATP and CCSSO staff, with technical assistance from Joe Crawford of CCSSO.

Public comments on the final draft were collected from various stakeholders and potential users for a period of 55 days. Again, CCSSO's online management tool was utilized to collect and analyze all public comments, both positive and negative. A consensus process was employed by the WG to determine how to react to, integrate, and/or use these comments. Once the WG completed its analysis of all public comments and made its final recommendations on revisions to the final draft, the Sponsors considered the entire package of documentation before adopting this new version of the *Operational Best Practices*.

## Use of the Document

Several caveats accompany the publication of the 2013 edition of the *Operational Best Practices*; these are virtually identical to those applicable to the 2010 edition and are intended to guide readers in the proper use and interpretation of this document.

The Sponsors seek to strengthen public confidence in the accuracy and quality of testing data and their use in improving instruction and learning. The focus of these *Operational Best Practices* is on specific operational testing practices that have the potential to enhance the quality, accuracy, and timeliness of student test data derived from large-scale assessments used by states. The document also recognizes the separate, but interrelated and reciprocal, responsibilities of testing companies and states in implementing state testing programs that meet the needs of both states and publishers.

These best practices are voluntary and are not part of any federal or state statutory or regulatory requirements, nor do the Sponsors believe they should be. Moreover, implementation of these best practices by testing companies and states is not an "all or nothing" proposition. Successful testing programs have been created and administered without each practice being employed. In reality, some practices may not be applicable in some settings, for some states, or under some circumstances. Accordingly, the Sponsors wish to emphasize that successful testing programs may not need to incorporate each and every practice or each and every component of a practice.

The Sponsors continue to believe that the state assessment program process will evolve as states and consortia of states wrestle with the challenging problems posed by Race to the Top, and as stakeholders focus on the reauthorized ESEA and its implementation requirements. For this reason, the online feedback procedure adopted in 2010 is being retained so that comments on the 2013 edition can be easily collected. The Sponsors encourage future users of the *Operational Best Practices* to submit their comments and suggestions for improving this work, so that the document can be maintained as needed in the future. [www.ccsso.org/best_practices_review].

## Terminology Used in the Document

A glossary of terms used in the *Operational Best Practices* is provided at the end of this document. However, because of the manner and frequency in which the following four terms are used in the document, the Working Group thought it was important to provide definitions in the Introduction, prior to provision of the specific chapters. The four terms are project manager, program manager, client, and service provider. The definition of how each of these terms is used in the document follows.

Project Manager: A project manager is the person assigned by the performing organization to achieve the project objective. According to the Program Management Institute (PMI), a project is a temporary endeavor undertaken to create a unique product, service, or result. For a statewide assessment, a project manager is generally responsible for delivery of one or more components of an assessment contract.

Program Manager: A program manager is the person assigned to coordinate and manage all elements of the program. According to PMI, a program is a group of related projects managed in a coordinated way to attain benefits and control not available from managing them individually. For a statewide assessment, program managers for the client and the service provider will be jointly responsible for the delivery of all components of an assessment contract.

Client: An entity that contracts for service. When applied in the large-scale assessment market, the client is typically a state department of education.

Service Provider: An entity that provides assessments and related services to the client. When applied in the large-scale assessment market, a service provider contracting directly with the client is typically considered to be a prime contractor, and is referred to as a contractor in this document. Other service providers contracting with the prime contractor to provide components of the overall contract are typically considered to be subcontractors, which is the term used in this document.

# PRE-CHAPTER. STATE CONSIDERATIONS FOR ASSESSMENT PROGRAM DESIGN

## Introduction

The assessment program design provides the foundation for development and implementation decisions to be made in a large-scale assessment program. The purpose of this chapter is to assist staff in departments of education to review best practices as they evaluate and make changes to current assessment programs, develop an entirely new assessment program, participate in assessment consortia and/or use the assets from a consortium. All decisions and planning will be subject to state procurement law, the state history, the legislative policy framework and the infrastructure or capacity of the field.

Ultimately, the program goals and purposes will be the primary factors guiding the final assessment program design, as decisions are made in assessment system development and implementation, including evaluations aimed at improving the interoperability of technology components and data/content exchange.

I.    **Program Design. Although the client initiating a change in the assessment program has the ultimate responsibility for the planning decisions, the client may, subject to state procurement laws, find it useful to obtain advice from existing service providers. One way to do this is through a Request for Information (RFI) or similar inquiry.**

II.   **Legislation and policy will provide the framework for the assessment program and design. A client may be responding to new legislation, transitioning to changed policy requirements, managing the impact of assessment consortium activities and products, or participating in a consortium of states for the development and implementation of an assessment program.**

II.a  As decision-making begins, the client (e.g. state's department of education) should have a clear understanding of the state's expectations and requirements. It is important to clarify the fundamental principles and purpose because these will guide the overall assessment design.

II.b    The client will need to consider the feasibility of execution and timeframe needed to meet the state and federal policy and legislative requirements.

II.c    The client must understand and consider such factors as: the limitations of end users' capacity, possible consortium structure, and industry best practices.

III.    **The purposes of the assessment program will guide its development and implementation. Consortia activities and requirements may also influence timing, implementation and service provider scope and involvement.**

III.a   The history of the client's assessment program design should be considered in making revisions to an existing system, developing a new assessment program, or the transitioning to a consortium system design.

III.b   Historical perspectives, past implementation, and the practicality of changes in assessment programs must be considered, and will influence implementation decisions about new assessment design, delivery, and the purpose of assessment.

III.c   The client must clearly understand and articulate the purposes of the new assessment design and the intended assessment data uses. These purposes may include, but are not limited to, providing data relevant to and appropriate for the following:

- state and/or federal accountability;
- student achievement of performance standards;
- instructional improvement;
- school improvement;
- teacher effectiveness;
- 3rd Party research; and
- integration with other data tools and resources.

III.d    In all cases, the purposes of the assessment program under development need to be clearly articulated in the assessment program design.

III.e    The client will need a plan that ensures that both short and long-term goals and tasks of the program are realistic, outlined, and delivered with clear timelines.

> III.e(i)    Short-term goals and tasks might include such things as transitioning tasks either from a previous vendor or from a previous program design, developing test specifications, item development, test construction, test administration and, in the case of technology-enhanced testing, platform construction, modification, and implementation.

> III.e(ii)    Long-term goals and tasks might include such things as reporting results, implementing data communication tools, and using data in formative or summative ways.

IV.    **Assessment Program Design. General design decisions will be determined by state procurement laws, policy, history, and assessment program goals. The general program design includes many components, such as content standards, testing modes, item types, psychometric models, test development and administration, scoring and reporting, and other program elements.**

IV.a    **Content standards.** Decisions about assessment program design will be based upon the client's content standards (e.g., the Common Core State Standards, standards for learning the English language), the constructs to be measured within those standards, and the achievement standards that describe levels of student performance. Additional information regarding item types is found in Chapter 2.

IV.b    **Assessment program components.** Decisions about how program components (e.g., formative, interim/benchmark, summative assessments, English Language Proficiency (ELP) assessments) integrate or coordinate need to be discussed.

IV.c **Testing modes.** Decisions about chosing paper-based or technology-based testing need to be considered with respect to financial, operational, information technology (IT) infrastructure impacts, diversity of student populations (e.g., range of language learning and disabilities), and assessment goals. The capacity of the state agency, districts, and schools must be considered. Client considerations may be constrained by varying factors and need to be evaluated relative to program goals. Further detail is provided throughout the book.

IV.d **Interoperability.** Decisions about the interoperability of systems, the exchange of content, data, and results, are critical considerations. Chapter 22 addresses the concept of interoperability and industry standards. Specific examples of the application of interoperability principles are found in Chapters 2, 3, 6 15, 17, 18, and 19.

IV.e **Item types.** The program design and mode of testing will determine item types. Item type decisions need to be thoroughly considered because there are many different types, delivered through both paper-based and technology-based modes. Additional information regarding item types and item banking is found in Chapters 2 and 3.

IV.f **Psychometric models.** Decisions about measurement models, including considerations such as field testing, scaling, equating, and standard setting, should be examined. All psychometric decisions must be consistent with industry standards, especially the *Joint Standards* in reference to professional scientific standards. Additional information regarding psychometric options is found in Chapters 4, 5, and 16.

IV.g **Test development.** Decisions about item development processes, item reviews (e.g., content, alignment, fairness and sensitivity), and test construction are important. Universal design must be considered throughout the test development process. Additional information is found in Chapters 2, 3, 4, 5, and 19.

IV.h **Test administration and scheduling.** Decisions about test administration must be considered in the assessment design. The administration schedule generally dictates the timeframe for all other tasks. The client should evaluate its comprehensive schedule for test development, test administration, scoring, and reporting. Planning will need to include timelines for state and federal accountability. The schedule and training for test administration needs to be evaluated, and a plan for communicating the eventual schedule and training needs to be considered. Additional information is found in Chapters 9, 10, 11, and 12.

IV.i **Scoring and reporting.** Decisions are primarily dependent upon the program goals, assessment purposes (e.g., summative, interim), and use of performance data. Fundamental differences exist between scoring and reporting of paper-based and technology-based assessments and should be considered in decision-making. Additional information is found in Chapters 13, 14, and 15.

V. **Technology. Decisions about the assessment program design, including accessibility for diverse student populations, will drive the technology requirements needed to support the program. The successful adoption of technology-based assessments requires evaluation of current and emerging technology for operational capabilities, as well as consideration of system interoperability.**

V.a **Infrastructure.** The client will need to consider the readiness of existing local and state technology infrastructure. The client will need to be aware of and communicate the minimum technology requirements to successfully support the defined program design goals.

V.b **Methodology.** The client will need to consider establishing a process for implementing appropriate methodology, for evaluating current local site readiness, and for planning for emerging technology requirements.

V.c **Systems interoperability.** The client will need to consider the goals and benefits of interoperability, including the use of available industry standards, at the initial point of program design. Putting in place interoperable solutions may benefit the assessment program by enabling enhancements or simply providing more efficient transitions from one service provider's solution (either hardware, software, or both) to another service provider's solution (see Chapter 22).

V.d    **Data integration and resources.** The client will need to consider its goals for integrated data warehousing, management, and reporting as part of technology planning to support the program. Integration efforts along with existing and new systems development will be needed. These efforts should all be considered, as part of the client's overall assessment program, while supporting systems and infrastructure are developed, interoperable solutions are evaluated, and data management objectives set (see Chapters 18 and 22).

V.e    **Sustainability and interoperability.** The client will need to consider future plans to sustain and manage technology platforms, systems and infrastructure components, including how best to achieve interoperability. Overall program goals, projected budgets, and implementation timelines will influence and guide client requirements (see Chapter 22).

V.f    **Training.** The client will need to consider establishing a plan for training, including such elements as format, participants, and logistics (see Chapters 1, 8, 9, 14, and as referenced in other chapters). Training also should include technical and administrative training on relevant test administration processes for all stakeholders.

VI.    **Security. Increased awareness of security issues, increased public scrutiny of testing practices, and the value of strong security practices in the proper uses of test results make it important to evaluate a state's security policies and practices. A comprehensive security plan should cover such topics as security policies, legal support, identification of threats and** vulnerabilities, and how to respond to security incidents. Best practices on these topics and others are found in Chapters 8, 9, and 15, and are noted in other chapters.

VII.   **Accessibility and Accommodations. Accessibility and accommodations design considerations must be guided by state and federal legislative requirements. Accessibility needs should be informed by principles of universal design. Allowable accommodations need to be clearly defined and communicated, and then evaluated on a periodic basis. Additional information is available in Chapter 19.**

VIII.   **Data Management Decisions. The client will need to consider decisions regarding data management. Additional information is found in Chapter 18.**

    VIII.a   The steps in the collection and management of data will vary depending upon infrastructure and capacity. Additionally, reporting requirements may impact how data are managed and used.

    VIII.b   Rules, procedures, and a communication plan need to be established to assure data quality, security, and management.

    VIII.c   Decisions for enabling data interoperability will provide more flexibility in managing data throughout the assessment program (see Chapter 22).

IX.   **Roles and Responsibilities. Decisions about the roles and responsibilities of the client and service providers will need to be established and documented. Additional information is found in Chapters 1 and 7.**

    IX.a   The assignment of roles and responsibilities may vary between the client and the service provider(s) as documented in the applicable contract(s). For example, the client and the service provider(s) may share responsibilities for the development of the assessment program, professional development, materials preparation, and/or customer service.

    IX.b   If consortia arrangements and responsibilities are included in the planning discussions, the roles of all parties need to be defined, agreed upon, and communicated to all parties.

X.  **Budget. Decisions about budget must be considered and determined by the client.**

    X.a    The client should prioritize budgetary considerations such as resources, capabilities, and training.

    X.b    Procedures for managing changes in scope must be articulated, documented, and applied.

XI.  **Procurement. After gathering and evaluating design, development, and implementation requirements, the client will, in accord with procurement laws, issue a Request for Proposal (RFP) or similar document (see Chapter 20). The RFP should contain sufficient information to allow all qualified service providers to understand the scope and specifications of the program being sought.**

# CHAPTER 1.  PROGRAM MANAGEMENT AND CUSTOMER SERVICE

## Introduction

The use of proven program management best practices is central to the successful implementation of a statewide large-scale assessment program. The role of the service provider's program manager is to ensure that all deliverables (e.g., products, technologies, services, related materials, and documentation) specified in the contract are of high quality, meet customer requirements, and are delivered on schedule and within budget. This is true whether the program provides paper test booklets, technology-based test delivery, or mixed-mode testing. The equally important role of the client's program manager is to oversee all aspects of the contract from the client's perspective, ensure that the program development and implementation are functioning smoothly and efficiently, and respond to questions from the service provider's program manager.

To effectively create and operate a statewide assessment program requires a collaborative partnership between a client program manager, a service provider program manager, and, in a technology-based assessment program, leaders on both teams with expertise in technology. Together the managers and team leaders should coordinate and implement core components of an effective program management approach. This will ensure that all requirements of the client's program are met. These components should include, at a minimum, agreed-upon processes and protocols for:

- scope definition and client requirements;
- cost management;
- program transitioning, including any interoperability evaluations and solutions;
- communication, meetings, and status reporting;
- scope change control;
- staffing changes;
- expectations for working with and training the local education agencies (LEAs) and schools/districts within state;

- necessary components of a technology-based testing environment (if applicable); and
- any additional components that may be added with the agreement of both parties.

The program should meet stakeholders' expectations whether tests are paper-based, technology-based, or delivered in a mixed-mode environment. The use of program management best practices in these areas should help ensure the implementation and administration of a successful quality program.

1.1 **The service provider and the client will each appoint an individual to serve as its program manager. A manager should be supported by a team of experts in order to implement the assessment program design (see Pre-Chapter State Checklist). The responsibilities of the program managers for each party include the following:**

- overseeing the full scope of project;

- overseeing budget and invoicing, including initiation and oversight of scope changes;

- developing and communicating procedures and protocols for each mode of testing being designed;

- ensuring the quality of the technology-based assessment requirements (if part of the design) including, but not limited to, issues of technology, network infrastructure, connectivity, security, software, test administration, accommodations, contingency plans, and customer service;

- overseeing implementation and execution of the technology readiness plan, including training and support of both technical and test administration personnel at all participating sites;

- addressing potential problems in a proactive manner and promptly resolving existing problems in all testing modes, including evaluation of the interoperability of existing system components and accessibility of assessments;

- developing agenda topics for all meetings involving both parties;

- developing an agreed upon schedule and ensuring all timelines and milestones are met for all deliverables in all testing modes;

- establishing and implementing the chain of decision making within both parties;

- ensuring clear communication between both parties at all levels; and

- ensuring all deliverables for all testing modes required under the contract are accurate, complete, and timely.

1.2 **The program managers for the service provider and the client should have a clear understanding of the scope and costs of the program. The program managers should have an understanding about the contract requirements of the assessment program design and promptly disclose any issues that may jeopardize the success of the program.**

1.3 **Program managers for the client and the service provider should work collaboratively and establish a team approach.**

1.4 **A process will be established for identifying the required program management qualifications for the desired assessment program design and each segment of the contractual requirements.**

    1.4.1 Both the service provider and the client each should prepare a list of qualifications for its program manager and should jointly review these lists of required qualifications. Qualifications should address the following:

- certification(s) required;

- educational background and experience;

- large-scale assessment experience;

- experience in meeting unique client specifications as outlined in the assessment program design; and

- other experience required (e.g., technology-based testing, assessment security, systems interoperability, assessing special populations/subgroups, content development, content standards).

1.4.2   Based on satisfaction of qualifications and the proposed assessment program design, the service provider and the client should identify their respective program managers.

**1.5   A program planning meeting with key client and service provider staff should be conducted before starting a new program or between program years. Program transitions or specific assessment program design plans may require meetings to be held prior to the initial meeting (see Chapter 21). It is strongly recommended that subsequent meetings occur at least semi-annually.**

1.5.1   Agendas for meetings should be developed jointly by the service provider and the client. The agenda for each meeting should include at least the following:

- discussion points related to current deliverables and milestones of the assessment program design;

- updates to key staff assignments and changes in responsibilities;

- new issues arising since the last meeting; and

- other information or issues related to the program managers' duties.

1.5.2   A set of specifications for meeting logistics should be developed, including tracking of decisions and action items, audiences for communications, and any other required protocols.

1.5.3   Both parties should include the appropriate team leaders and technology experts.

1.5.4   Minutes of meetings should be kept and provided to all participants in a timely fashion.

1.5.5   Documentation of scope of work and program specification requirements should be developed and made available to all attendees. This documentation should be in accord with the assessment program design and include the following:

- annual program schedule;

- service provider milestones;

- specified key dates;

- roles and responsibilities of key staff;

- materials lists associated with milestones of the assessment program design;

- lists of deliverables and handoffs associated with milestones; and

- evaluation of current and/or previous project implementation, outstanding issues, and/or a risk analysis plan, including mitigation activities, if applicable.

1.5.6  The client should provide a clear description of the assessment program information and implementation requirements, including any modifications for the upcoming assessment cycle. Both the service provider and the client should agree upon a schedule for delivery of products, technologies, services, documentation and the requirements and specifications of technology-based testing, if included in the program design. This documentation should include specifications for provision of the following:

- student background and demographic information;

- student enrollment information;

- school addresses and relevant school information;

- district database information, including addresses, and relevant staff and contact information;

- school database information, class assignments, accessibility requirements, use of accommodations, and any other student profile information;

- transfer and security of electronic student data files and communication protocols for their transfer;

- procedures for the corrections of student information and of electronic files shared between the service provider and the client;

- requirements for paper document and electronic file retention (e.g., student responses, district enrollment information);

- systems interoperability requirements and communication protocols for the transfer of data and other information between the client, the service provider, and districts/schools; and

- the proposed schedule for testing.

1.6 **Protocols should be established between the client and the service provider to help ensure communication between the parties. These protocols should address the following and include all aspects of the assessment program design, including information technology considerations, if applicable:**

- chain of decisions;

- communications plan;

- status reports;

- planning agendas;

- meeting minutes;

- conference calls at set intervals;

- milestone meetings or other meetings at set intervals as specified by contract; and

- scope changes.

1.7 **A separate protocol may need to be developed to identify changes to the scope and/or schedule of the original assessment program design (including interoperability considerations) and the contract. The protocol should determine how the revised scope should be managed from both fulfillment (service/delivery of both paper-based and technology-based assessments) and business perspectives.**

1.7.1   Identification of a change in scope that requires a contract modification should be a shared responsibility of both the client and the service provider.

1.7.2   Program management staff (for both service provider and client) should discuss the change and seek agreement and approval of the new scope of work.

1.7.3   If a scope change requires specific expertise, then the program management staff should be adjusted to support the level of expertise required.

1.7.4   If a change request is made and the client and the service provider agree upon a new or changed scope of work, the service provider should present the client with a written proposal or addendum to the contract setting forth terms of the new scope of work. This proposal/ addendum should include information on the following:

- changes in deliverables or new deliverables;

- modifications or updates to the schedule; and

- costs associated with change request.

1.7.5   A change management process should be defined to address the evolution of an interoperability approach in response to changes in technology requirements, contract changes, and/or standards definitions. Additionally, the client and the service provider should define a plan to include monitoring and participating within the standards community working groups, and attending conferences.

1.7.6   The client should approve the service provider's proposal before work commences, subject to terms of the contract.

1.7.7   If extenuating circumstances require that work begin before a scope change process can be completed, a "work-at-risk" protocol should be put into place. This protocol should describe how work can be started prior to contract adjustments and clearly articulate risks and responsibilities for all parties involved. If state procurement law prohibits "work-at-risk," that limitation needs to be communicated to the service provider and its impact clearly explained.

**1.8**  **A procedure for handling staffing changes will be developed and agreed upon by the client and the service provider. To the extent possible, adequate notice should be given so that a replacement can be named in a timely fashion.**

> 1.8.1  A procedure should be established for dealing with the situation where a key staff member becomes unavailable to serve the program. This could occur for many reasons, including voluntary or involuntary termination, medical leave, or change in job status. This procedure should address the following:
>
> - identifying an individual's replacement (ensuring the person meets all qualifications and expertise);
>
> - appropriate early and full disclosure regarding communication of any replacements; and
>
> - a plan to help the replacement become integrated into the program as soon as possible, preferably with some overlap, to provide a smooth transition.
>
> 1.8.2  A plan for documentation and key resource transfer should be developed to help ensure a smooth transfer of personnel for either the client or the service provider.

**1.9**  **The client will have overall responsibility for and will work with the service provider to establish and maintain a working relationship with the districts and schools within the state. This relationship should include protocols for:**

- communication (e.g., who contacts districts to follow up on any identified action);

- distribution, administration, and collection of assessment materials;

- technology-based implementation planning and execution, if part of assessment program design;

- distribution and management of technology-based assessment training (e.g., on security and test administration) and support documentation and tools, if applicable (see Chapters 8 and 9);

- electronic exchange of data (see Chapter 18);

- implementation of a customer service and support plan;

- working one-on-one with districts and schools in problem solving technical and interoperability issues, especially if technology-based assessments are included in the assessment program design; and

- providing assistance, when covered in the contract and as agreed upon and feasible, in response to security breaches within a district and/or school (see Chapter 8).

1.10 The service provider will update the client with progress reports that are timely and well documented. The client will notify the service provider in advance, to the extent possible, of any extenuating circumstances that might cause delays.

1.11 The service provider will manage and be responsible for all subcontractors it uses for the program per the client's procurement laws and contract requirements.

1.12 Processes will be established to help ensure the quality of information provided to clients or school/district representatives by customer service, program support representatives, and through self-serve informational websites, as appropriate.

1.12.1 Quality assurance methods for customer service and support should be developed to help ensure accuracy and reliability of information.

1.12.2 Ongoing training of customer service representatives should be conducted to help ensure they possess the most up-to-date information and technical expertise.

1.12.3 Processes should be established to help ensure consistent messaging regarding products, procedures, and processes if/when multiple customer service and support representatives are communicating with clients or school/district representatives.

1.13 Processes will be established to help ensure client requests are processed accurately and in a timely manner.

1.13.1 A process for tracking uncompleted orders, client requests, or issues should be established and information provided on a daily or other regular basis to customer service and program support management to help ensure that client-related issues are not neglected.

1.13.2 A document retention process should be created for orders, client requests, and issues that are received via online, data transfer, fax, e-mail, or mail.

1.13.3 Processes should be agreed upon for client review and acceptance of deliverables prior to broad implementation, where applicable.

1.13.4 Processes should be established for handling the client's technical inquiries, including about testing processes, responsively and in a timely manner.

1.13.5 Documents should be reviewed on a daily basis by customer service and support representatives to determine any order, client request, or issue that can be or has been solved or corrected.

1.13.6 Process updates should be provided to reflect administration work requests (e.g., class rosters, scheduling, invalidations) either through reports or self-service client access.

1.13.7 Retention processes and protocols for student answer documents, test booklets, and responses to technology-based assessments should be defined.

1.13.8 Processes and protocols should be defined for handling complaints and concerns regarding testing procedures (for all delivery methods). These should include monitoring, documenting, and communicating complaints by customer service and support representatives to determine the need for escalation and resolution.

**1.14 Processes will be established to facilitate an orderly transition of verbal or written communication from the customer service or support system to other departments within the service provider's organization.**

1.15 **Processes will be established to help ensure that material and communication security is enforced for both paper-based and technology-based testing processes and so that confidentiality is maintained.**

  1.15.1 Processes and protocols should be established for reporting, documenting, and resolving testing irregularities, including breaches of security.

  1.15.2 This is especially important when resolving issues related to materials on secure materials lists or issues involving student identification information or individual student results.

1.16 **Customer service or support functions may not always follow the service provider's standard processes. This divergence may be due to unique client requirements of the assessment program design, as articulated via the contract or the request for proposal (RFP) process. In such cases, processes should be established for identifying staffing requirements and modifications necessary to meet the client needs.**

  1.16.1 It is critical that if the assessment program design includes a mixed mode, the program managers work to assure alignment among all modes of testing.

  1.16.2 The client should inquire about, leverage, and use, where practicable, existing service provider standard customer service, technology infrastructure, and support processes.

  1.16.3 Using existing services should yield economies of scale and make the best use of cumulative history and experience of the service provider.

1.17 **After each testing cycle, the client and the service provider should conduct a review documenting lessons learned and establishing improvement plans.**

# CHAPTER 2. ITEM DEVELOPMENT

## Introduction

An assessment cycle should begin with clearly defined test specification documents that enable the development of test items, whether they are being developed for high-stakes or for lower-stakes assessments. These specifications define the item types (e.g., multiple choice, short answer, constructed response, performance task, technology-enhanced items such as drag-and-drop, hot-spot, simulation) and coverage of grade level, course, and content, based on the state's or program's content standards. Using well-defined test specifications, items are developed and reviewed through processes adopted by the client, including the use of universal design principles so that, to the extent feasible, items are developed for all student populations (e.g., all student subgroups, including students with disabilities, English learners [ELs], and ELs with disabilities).

The assessment cycle might include provisions for continuing item development cycles, if specified by the assessment program design. If the testing program is currently paper-based, consideration should be given to the possibility of a transition to technology-based assessments, as well as a focus on how interoperability would improve the item development process.

**2.1 Test specifications describing attributes of the assessment should be developed for each grade and content area prior to the development of assessment items and related ancillary materials.**

    2.1.1   Prior to the beginning of development activities, the client should provide the service provider with the state or program academic content standards, along with the corresponding curricular frameworks and benchmarks, and, where appropriate, standards for learning the English language.

            The client should also provide the service provider with the measurement model specifications, the passage or stimulus selection guidelines, the performance level descriptors, and, if used, the style guide and other relevant documents.

2.1.2     As described in the contract, the client and the service provider should define and confirm the details of the test specifications, understanding that these may change over time at the direction of the client. These specifications may include the following:

- the test design (e.g., numbers of items, formats of items, numbers of passages/stimuli, numbers of forms, distributions of item types, use of supporting materials like formula sheets, calculators);

- the need, if any, for alternative assessment forms (e.g., braille, large-print, Spanish language) or alternate assessments for special populations (e.g., Alternate Assessment based on Alternate Achievement Standards [AA-AAS]), either for paper-based or technology-based delivery;

- the test blueprint for each grade and content area (e.g., coverage of curriculum frameworks and benchmarks, often manifested as numbers, ranges, or percentages of test items per standard or benchmark);

- the layout specifications for technology-based items (e.g., transition from item to item, arrangement of items on screen, use of color, font sizes);

- a plan to reflect item equivalents for dual modes, if applicable. This plan should reflect item-format and item-quantity requirements (e.g., some technology-based item types do not have an equivalent format in paper and pencil);

- paper-based test versions as an accommodation when an assessment is technology-based;

- specifications for computer-adaptive testing (CAT) and linear-on-the-fly testing (LOFT), including item presentation algorithms, minimum blueprint and subscore criteria, item pool ratios of items to blueprint, and the termination criteria; and

- the item development plan, which may include the following elements:

  - numbers of items to be developed;

  - process for development of test items;

  - acceptability of cloned or template-generated items;

  - item prototype development;

  - process for passage acquisition;

  - definition of item development specifications;

  - the client's accommodations policy and/or allowable accommodations; and

  - item review procedures, schedules, quantities, and quality acceptance criteria.

2.1.3   The service provider and the client should define the details of item specifications in the context of the construct(s) being assessed. Item specifications may include the following:

- requirements for application of universal design principles;

- content to be tested (e.g., content standards, learning progressions);

- construct definitions, including relevant and irrelevant factors;

- item type(s) to be employed;

- requirements for developing scoring rules for constructed-response and technology-enhanced items, as applicable;

- linguistic difficulty;

- cognitive complexity;

- item difficulty;

- reading levels and/or text complexity of reading passages and other text-based stimuli;

- attendance to varying levels of student achievement;

- suitability of access for special populations;

- use of graphics, tables, charts, etc.; and

- full details about how technology-enhanced items function.

2.1.4   The service provider and the client should define the specifications and options for technology-based delivery of test items, as applicable, including such issues as navigation of passages and other stimuli, use of technology-based tools (e.g., calculator, protractor), use of screen real estate, use of reference sheets, navigation features provided to students, use of audio capability and variability of delivery (e.g., speed, pausing, restarting), acceptable graphic/video format specifications (e.g., .jpg, .gif, .avi, .wmv, .swf, .mov), screen resolution, use of color, size of text, and graphics.

**2.2   A timeline for the development of test items should be established and agreed upon by the service provider and the client.**

2.2.1   Revisions to the timeline should be agreed upon by the service provider and the client, and a process for establishing changes to the timeline should be specified in advance.

2.2.2   The agreed-upon timeline should be adhered to by both parties.

**2.3   The client and the service provider will specify an item development process, including editorial procedures. This process should cover some or all of the following:**

- procedures for improving interoperability of item content exchanges, including, where appropriate, item development and item reviews;

- specifications for the source of the items to be developed, whether by in-state educators, experts supplied by the service provider, a combination of these sources, or other sources;

- the method for authoring the items, indirectly (to be entered into a system later), or directly into an item banking system;

- specifications for authoring technology-enhanced items, including templates and/or storyboard requirements;

- provisions for determining that items are developed by individuals with expertise in the content area for which items are being developed;

- definition of content and editorial review cycles;

- fairness and sensitivity review procedures;

- defined reviews for the level of accessibility for special populations and allowable accommodations; and

- the method for final approval and signoff by all identified parties.

2.4 Depending on the contract, the client or the service provider may procure an independent external expert review (e.g., a review by professional scientists or historians) of parts of the program, including such aspects as test or item specifications, items, test forms, and braille forms. The client and the service provider should consider the qualification and selection of reviewers, criteria for reviews, and the resolution process for obtaining final results.

2.5 The service provider should conduct internal reviews of draft items prior to their final inclusion, checking for some or all of the following, as agreed upon by the client:

- alignment to standards and curricular frameworks derived from content standards (e.g., standards for learning the English language);

- alignment to appropriate level of cognitive and language complexity;

- compliance with item specifications;

- accuracy of keyed correct responses;

- plausibility (and incorrectness) of distracters;

- reasonableness and completeness of the scoring rubrics for constructed-response (CR) items;

- reasonableness and completeness of the scoring rules for technology-enhanced items, if required;

- rules for the use of artificial intelligence scoring functionality, as applicable;

- grade appropriateness;

- accuracy and completeness of diagrams, tables, graphics, etc;

- usability of technology-based presentation (e.g. navigation, placement of item elements);

- editorial accuracy;

- fairness and sensitivity issues;

- level of accessibility for special populations, including defined allowable accommodations; and

- appropriateness of alternative assessment forms (e.g., braille, large-print, Spanish language), or alternate assessments (e.g., Alternate Assessment based on Alternate Achievement Standards [AA-AAS]).

**2.6** **A process should be established by the service provider and the client to guide and track revisions and rewrites that may be exchanged between any two parties in the development process.**

**2.7** **The client will specify program requirements for passages, written materials, graphics, photographs, and other related item stimuli. These requirements may determine the need for permissions and rights solicitations. These requirements should include:**

- specifications for published versus commissioned materials;

- sources of commissioned materials, if used;

- requirements for obtaining permission for use of third-party materials, if used, including number of years for permissions and terms of use;

- requirements for item release, including posting on the Internet;

- administration details for field and/or operational testing; and

- location and format of source files for graphics.

**2.8** **The client and the service provider will define an overall item review process and acceptance criteria. This process should cover the following areas:**

- client review prior to committee review;

- committee and/or department review protocols;

- post-committee protocols;

- version control of items by the service provider as items move through review (provided by an item authoring and banking system, where available);

- item bank analysis and inventory by the service provider to determine areas of needed item/passage development, as defined by the program test blueprint, before new development begins; and

- acceptance rate of items by standard, content area, and grade, cognitive level, etc.

**2.9** **The service provider and the client will conduct committee reviews facilitated by client and/or service provider staff. For each committee, there should be a clear description of its purpose and its contribution to the overall development process, and training should be provided to the committee members by the client and/or the service provider. Committee reviews may include the following, as appropriate:**

- item passage and scenario review;

- item content review committee;

- fairness and sensitivity review;

- item data review; and

- other reviews required by the program.

**2.10** **The client will identify members of each review committee and/or the requirements the service provider will follow for soliciting and securing appropriate committee members. Committees may be convened by grade and content area or committees may include multiple grades and/or multiple content areas.**

    2.10.1  Requirements for committee selection, the process for securing committee members, and the results of such a process should be documented when appropriate, including the following:

- target committee attributes, if known or desired;

- relevant demographics, and other committee selection characteristics (e.g., school district or constituency represented by committee member, familiarity with technology-based assessment); and

- comparison of final committee makeup against any relevant target goals, including notation of differences, if any.

    2.10.2  The service provider should furnish item analysis information to the client and review committees as agreed upon by contract. When sample size permits, such data should be provided for appropriate subgroups, including special populations. Item analysis information may include:

- response option distributions;

- percentile analysis (e.g., quartile analysis);

- item discrimination information (e.g., biserial correlations);

- item difficulty information;

- measurement model fit;

- differential item functioning (DIF); and

- distributions of response latencies for computer administered items, as appropriate.

2.10.3  The number of committee meetings required or desired should be identified. Both the client and the service provider should work to ensure that costs, schedule, security procedures, and requirements for committee meetings are part of the contract, statement of work, or RFP.

2.10.4  The service provider and the client should reach an agreement on who will facilitate committee meetings and how they will be facilitated.

2.10.5  Specific roles and responsibilities of staff from both the client and the service provider should be determined prior to committee meetings. These roles and responsibilities should be documented and communicated.

2.10.6  Contingency plans should be developed. These should include procedures that the client or service provider staff can follow in the event of a committee meeting disruption (e.g., power outage, fire drill, or other unforeseen facility issue), disruptive committee member, security breach when secure materials are being reviewed, failure of committee or staff members to attend the meeting, or errors in printed materials.

2.10.7  Expense reimbursement and honorarium payment procedures should be established, documented, and communicated to the client and the service provider staff as well as to committee members.

2.10.8  Materials for committee review, facility logistics, and check-in/verification procedures should be established and distributed ahead of time.

2.10.9　For site-based review, meeting rooms should be arranged to optimize committee interaction. When possible, nonsecure materials should be distributed within meeting rooms prior to committee arrival.

2.10.10 For virtual reviews, the technology and security requirements should be distributed to the committee participants prior to the meeting. Overall meeting security, as well as the security of reviewed materials, should be determined. Reviews themselves may be conducted either in a group setting or by reviewers individually. If reviewers work individually, the client and the service provider should agree on methods of reconciliation and signoff. Appropriate support should be made available to participants for access during meetings (see Chapter 8).

2.10.11 All items should be presented to reviewers as faithfully to the student's experience as possible.

**2.11　The client and the service provider should develop, document, and implement procedures for improving the interoperability of assessment item content, including, where appropriate, item development and item reviews.**

2.11.1　The client and the service provider should evaluate the interoperability of all solutions that are used to import and export item content using an appropriate industry standard when the program has a need to move item content between service providers, systems, or users, (e.g., sharing items for review, transitioning items from development to test publishing, or releasing items from a high-stakes program for local use or to the public).

2.11.2　In defining assessment item content interoperability for the program, the client and the service provider should evaluate available industry standards (see Chapter 22) and should implement a standard that addresses the following areas:

2.11.2.1　Item content. The item content standard should be flexible enough to support a variety of item types, representations, response structures, "reusability" across assessment delivery systems, and feedback documentation (e.g., content, bias, cognitive labs) at the item and/or distracter levels.

2.11.2.2 Legacy content format. Existing item banking systems may not use eXtensible Markup Language (XML) to present data; however, the use of XML has become more common. The client and the service provider should determine what format is used in current item banks for storing items (e.g., PDF, InDesign, MS Word) and whether the files contain original art work, so that it is possible and/or feasible to migrate existing item banks into XML-based standards.

2.11.2.3 Item types. It is common for technology standards to support the traditional item types (e.g., multiple-choice, true/false, drag-and-drop), but some standards do not support innovative or technology-enhanced items in an interoperable fashion. The client and the service provider should determine how applicable item types are supported, and how the use of available standards would affect interoperability of that content.

2.11.2.4 Scoring meta-data. The client and the service provider should consider if the interoperability standard being used defines item elements (e.g., correct responses, rubrics, or other scoring rules for each item), as well as considering whether scoring rules can be defined that match all of the types of items that are being used, and whether items can be identified as scored items, sample items, or field-test items.

2.11.2.5 Accessibility elements. The client and the service provider should agree on accessibility options for specific subgroups (e.g., read-aloud, large print, braille, page overlay, use of calculator) (see Chapter 19) and whether any available standards for such options meet the goals and objectives of the program, and how such options would be verified in the content review process. The client and the service provider should consider the impact these elements will have on these content development processes and evaluate the challenges these standards may introduce for bringing legacy content up to the standard.

2.11.2.6 Shared item content. The client and the service provider should consider how the available standard supports supplementary content that is independent of the item content (e.g., reading passages, tables, charts, art work), whether needed content elements can be represented easily in the standard, and whether item and form standard definitions can "link to" these resources.

2.11.2.7 Multiple platform presentation. Independent of the item content, the client and the service provider should consider whether the available standard supports additional layout and presentation specifications that may be platform- or delivery-system specific (i.e., paper-based or technology-based delivery), and whether other platforms (e.g., mobile devices, iPads) may introduce other layout or presentation considerations, including templates, style guides, or other strategies for providing platform-specific presentation and layout.

2.11.2.8 Content alignment to state curriculum (e.g., common core content standards) and proficiency standards (e.g., standards for learning the English language). The client and the service provider should consider whether the assessment interoperability standards can meet the levels and structure of these standards, and if so, how to align assessment items and other shared item content to such standards, understanding that a given item may measure more than one standard.

2.11.2.9 Statistical meta-data. The client and the service provider should consider whether the standard has a representation of the necessary statistical measures and data for items, for how items are used on forms, and for tracking statistics between administrations of test forms.

# CHAPTER 3. ITEM BANKING

## Introduction

An item bank is a repository for crucial information regarding many aspects of an assessment program. This information is used for item evaluation, test form construction, legal defensibility, and planning for future item development efforts. Such a repository often contains more than just test items. An item bank may also contain stimulus materials, artwork, statistical data, administration history, or other meta-data that allow for the linking of test items and their disposition to many other aspects of the assessment program, including the client's accommodation policy.

An item banking system can refer to either an integrated system encompassing such activities as item authoring, maintenance, and test form construction, or it can refer to multiple systems integrated to cover the full spectrum of development work. When an "item bank" is a compilation of many disparate systems, they must be linked together to keep track of assessment items and associated collateral information. For example, artwork associated with a test item might be stored in a location separate from the text of the test item itself. Similarly, the statistical data might be stored in yet another separate location, but be linked to the test item in a number of systematic ways. Finally, information regarding fonts, formats, and other attributes of test items (meta-data) might be stored in yet another location. Therefore, keeping track of these pieces of information (whether they are found in a single file or stored in separate databases), and providing an interoperable solution for exchanging such content, is paramount in maintaining a successful program. The disposition of these assets must be known and understood for the appropriate hand-offs between the service provider and the client. Such data exchanges will require evaluation and resolution of interoperability issues (see Chapter 22).

This chapter outlines some of the considerations regarding best practices for establishing and maintaining linked assessment information, or item banks, including considerations of data interoperability, that are likely to lead to successful use in an assessment program.

**3.1 The item banking system should consist of, or provide access through integration or linking to, the following:**

- all items, passages, or other stimuli, art and graphics, and other required meta-data, along with relevant source citations;

- other supportive documents, such as:

  - scoring rubrics, criteria, or directions;

  - information on allowable accommodations;

  - pretesting collateral, such as checklists or preorganizers; and

  - required manipulatives;

- attributes of the assessment items, including electronic tagging, such as:

  - item status and/or the item state within the development lifecycle (e.g., new, pilot, raw, pending, review, field test, operational, retired);

  - item cluster, objective, or subdomain memberships;

  - information about shared passages, stimuli, graphics, artwork, voiced descriptions/text, or other similar linkages;

  - any item-to-item relationships, such as items that cannot appear in the same form of the test (e.g., versioned items, cloned items, parent/child items, items that provide keying/cluing to other items) and adapted language versions;

  - applicable modes of delivery;

  - applicable accommodations or accommodation limitations (e.g., Accessible Portable Item Protocol [APIP] tagging) (see Chapter 22 Appendix);

  - distribution rationales;

  - manipulative designation (e.g., calculator, ruler, protractor);

- technological requirements for delivery (e.g., screen size, resolution, plug-in); and

- design layout considerations (per delivery mode);

- item bank inventories by project, including target numbers, actual numbers, and development forecasting information (i.e., the number and types of items that should be included in future item writing and review cycles);

- alignment information, such as:

  - curriculum, content standards, learning progressions, benchmarks, and item (and associated collateral) measures; and

  - depth of knowledge required by item or other noncontent related classification taxonomy (e.g., Bloom's Revised Taxonomy);

- disposition, parameters, and attributes of items, stimuli, passages, and tasks, such as:

  - the item use history;

  - the date when the item was constructed;

  - the correct answer key, prototypical response set for constructed-response items;

  - rights and permissions for artwork, passages, or graphics;

  - native format files for rendering items/art (e.g., Quark, Indesign, Adobe Illustrator, XML);

  - development comments, modification history, and approvals;

  - the committee comments, reviews, actions, and/ or recommendations;

  - the statistical data from pilot tests, field tests, and all operational uses of the item;

- the item positioning within the test form or session (sequencing) for all pilot tests, field tests, and operational uses of the item;

- usage rules for the items (e.g., frequency of use per delivery mode, exposure ranges, retirement requirements, technology restrictions/requirements);

- the information regarding public release, including release date for items, passages, and all items associated with a passage if not in the original release;

- the expert reviewer comments, if provided for by contract, such as third-party review of the use of universal design principles or item alignment findings;

- the items not yet piloted or field tested but approved, as well as approved but untested reading passages, stimuli, and graphics (including original source file), or when this is not possible, clearly delineated item banking system links to the location of the passages, stimuli, and graphics;

- the items, attributes, and systems to allow for electronic creation of an item review card at any stage that contains item image and attributes; and

- the capability to facilitate operational item selection;

- relevant information on the following types of assessments:

  - portfolio assessments and their collateral;

  - paper-based assessments;

  - technology-based assessments;

  - alternative assessment forms or alternate assessments for students with disabilities;

  - assessments for English learners (ELs);

  - formative assessment applicability; and

–  assessments adapted to multiple languages,
including the English language version of the item,
particularly if the source resides in the same item
banking system.

**3.2  The item bank should be made available to the client, as
agreed upon by the client and the service provider. Various
considerations may impact this accessibility.**

3.2.1  Procedures and processes for item bank use by the client
(and any subcontractors of the service provider) should be
established and documented as part of the contract. The
following areas should be covered:

- technology requirements;

- item format disposition at the end of the contract,
  when applicable (e.g., XML format, PDF format, or
  other accessible formats when the item bank is in the
  proprietary custody of the service provider); and

- training needs, schedules, and procedures.

3.2.2  Procedures and processes for item bank security when
used by the client (and any subcontractor of the service
provider) should be established and documented as part
of the contract. The following areas should be covered:

- roles and responsibilities of each party (e.g., client,
  vendor, subcontractors, external subject-matter experts);

- access timeframe and rights associated with each user
  role. Access levels may include one of the following:

  – full access, which includes the ability to view
    and edit all aspects of the system (e.g., item
    text, ancillary item information such as artwork,
    examination forms);

  – limited access, which provides access to
    particular components within the item banking
    system for viewing and editing purposes;

- read-only access, where viewing access is granted only to components within the system with no editing capabilities; and

- item bank use and security training by role and responsibilities for monitoring and maintaining appropriate user rights, including termination of rights, as determined by the client and the service provider, where the party responsible for maintenance of user rights would make decisions based on a number of factors, including who owns the item bank, who maintains custody of the item bank during the length of the contract, agreed upon security roles, etc. (see Chapter 8).

3.2.3 Procedures and processes for improving interoperability for item banking functions used by the client (and all subcontractors of the service provider) should be established and documented as part of the contract (see Chapter 22).

3.2.4 The client and the service provider should evaluate how available industry standards support supplementary content that is associated with the item content (e.g., reading passages, tables, charts, art work), whether needed content elements can be represented easily in the standard, and whether item and form standard definitions can "link to" these resources to support an item bank.

**3.3 Responsibility for maintenance and oversight of the item bank should be identified and agreed upon by all parties.**

3.3.1 Roles and responsibilities regarding maintenance of the ongoing item banking system should be established and documented.

3.3.2 Responsibility should be established and documented for maintaining and, when necessary, upgrading software and hardware required to view technology-enhanced items in the same format in which they are rendered for the student.

3.3.3   Procedures for routine item bank maintenance (e.g., importing of data, items, or other stimuli) should be established, agreed upon by both the client and the service provider, and should include the following:

- a schedule of when and how new content, data, standards, or other rules of the assessment program will be added to the item banking system;

- a schedule of item disposition to the client (e.g., yearly transfer of items to the client if they are the property of the client, as defined in the contract);

- version control processes to help ensure appropriate links to meta-data; and

- ongoing processes for update/refreshment of item bank inventories, including tracking and reporting to the client, when applicable.

3.3.4   The item bank should be maintained in a controlled, secure environment and should adhere to all applicable security requirements agreed upon by the client and the service provider, or as set forth elsewhere in this document (see Chapter 8).

3.3.5   The item bank should be accessible through a secure interface from remote locations rather than solely from installed computers at the client's site.

**3.4   Ownership of the item bank content, data, and attributes (e.g., items, statistical data, supporting documents, meta-data) should be specified, and documented in the contract (see Chapter 20).**

# CHAPTER 4. TEST CONSTRUCTION AND DEVELOPMENT

## Introduction

Once the item development cycle is completed, operational items are selected for use in various test designs, such as fixed forms or in pool-based testing (e.g., item-level adaptive using computer adaptive testing [CAT], multistage adaptive, and linear-on-the-fly-testing [LOFT]). The selection process identifies items that comply with item and test specifications, layout requirements (for paper and/or electronic delivery), and appropriate psychometric considerations. Specifications for both test and answer document design are developed and reviewed regularly. Using identified selection criteria, the client reviews and approves the selected operational items and field-test items, usually in collaboration with the service provider.

Production of assessment materials begins once the final items have been selected. Tests are arranged using agreed-upon production guidelines and protocols guided by the principles of universal design. For items requiring manipulatives (e.g., protractors, spinners, rulers, number blocks, scratch paper, balance scales, graph paper), the specifications are defined during the test development process, approved by the client, and then developed during the production cycle. The final version of the presentation of each item has been previously determined through the design, development and field testing processes. A test form specification provides direction on the selection and sequencing of items. Test design requirements may include: using a fixed set of items or pulling items from a larger set; specifying reviews; establishing time limits; providing instructions for item-level and test-level scoring and reporting; etc. The production process is characterized by various approval steps and may involve the transmission of documents and other files back-and-forth between the client and service providers. The result of the production process also makes the test available for test administration.

For paper-based assessment delivery, scannable answer documents are developed and constructed in conjunction with production of test booklets. The layout of the item response sections for answer documents follows the item flow of the test booklets, using agreed-upon labeling of multiple-choice response areas and allotting answer space for short-answer and constructed-response items as defined in the test specifications. For technology-based assessment delivery, the service provider uses the test specification along with all necessary files (e.g., items, answer keys, graphics, audio/video, meta-data, student answer section/area) to develop appropriate display and functionality on the platform for all students.

Requirements for special forms are defined by program needs as determined by the client. These may include paper or electronic braille forms, large print forms (technology-based or paper-based), forms in languages other than English (technology-based or paper-based), CDs, DVDs, videotapes, and other usable formats. The items contained in these forms or pools are also specified by the program. To the extent feasible, these special forms or pools should be developed at the same time as the targeted main assessment form. For information about accessibility of forms see Chapter 19.

**4.1    In order to place items on a fixed form or in a testing pool, the procedures, processes, responsibilities, and timelines should be established and implemented for selecting operational items, passages, graphics, artwork, stimulus materials, manipulatives, and/or other assessment collateral.**

    4.1.1    Because of rights and permissions issues, selection of passages, artwork, and/or graphics needs to be conducted early in the process for each delivery mode. Regardless of when it is conducted, procedures, processes, and responsibilities should be clearly delineated and documented.

    4.1.2    Procedures, processes, responsibilities, and timelines for reviews, verifications and approvals of test content and accessibility should be established and implemented using test development specifications. These procedures should cover the following:

- identification of the number and types of reviews or stages of review;

- identification of reviewers from the client's staff, the service provider's staff, and/or others;

- specification of the chain of authority regarding required and documented approval sign-offs;

- identification of procedures to help ensure security during review and approval process; and

- determination of action plans for when items or other selected content are not approved and must be replaced, including schedule impacts and risk assessment.

4.1.3   A timeline for test form development, reviews, modifications, and approval should be developed and agreed upon by the service provider and the client, which should contain:

- a well-defined timeline agreed to by both parties;

- a process for both parties to agree on any changes to the timeline; and

- a process for communicating unexpected delays by either the service provider or the client to the other party as soon as a delay is evident.

4.1.4   Specifications should include procedures and processes describing how to develop multiple forms for assessments that contain a core or common set of items, if applicable, along with many different versions or forms containing embedded field-test items, including alternative forms (e.g., braille, large print). Procedures should include specifications for how forms of a test containing field-test items, as defined by test development specifications, are constructed so that such field-test items blend as seamlessly as possible with the operational portion of the test.

. These procedures should ensure that:

- test forms follow the specified blueprint;

- test forms meet the established psychometric criteria;

- test forms should be similar (e.g., item sequencing, field test and anchor/equating item location, placement of graphics, accessibility), whether paper-based or technology-based;

- items used on all assessment forms are piloted and/or field tested in the format or formats in which they will be used operationally;

- items intended to be in used in technology-based assessments are piloted with the same presentation design, layout specifications, and available tools (highlighter, magnifying glass, ruler, etc.) that will be present in the operational forms;

- items intended to be used in technology-based assessments should be piloted with the same delivery rules (e.g., marking items, skipping items, reviewing items) that will be present in the operational forms; and

- items that were rejected or released are not included on the forms.

4.1.5    Test construction procedures should specify all statistical models used in the process.

**4.2    Procedures will be developed for coordinating production of test forms or item pool production, the selection of test items, the generation of multiple forms, and the production of the test forms (either paper-based or technology-based). These procedures should include:**

- requirements of materials manufacturing and electronic production, as outlined in Chapter 6;

- schedules for the review of materials that have been developed in collaboration with other contractors or vendors in determining production of test materials;

- agreed-upon paper or electronic formatting, layout (including font, white space, and other space requirements), and style guide requirements;

- agreed-upon procedures, processes, and timelines for review of final test forms or item pools (paper-based or technology-based) early enough in the production cycle to accommodate any identified defects; and

- agreed-upon procedures, processes, timelines, and requirements for generating supporting or ancillary materials, such as administrator manuals and other collateral.

**4.3 Test form development and/or item pool decisions for use of multistage, CAT or LOFT, will be a joint effort of the service provider and the client.**

**4.4 The following factors should be considered when specifying the layout of paper answer documents for students:**

- positioning of demographic data, as defined by data requirements;

- student characteristics (e.g., age and membership in special populations) and ability to indicate responses and use answer sheet formats;

- margins, marks, and image capture requirements, as specified in scanning documents;

- section breaks to match test booklet layout;

- for combined test booklet/answer documents, appropriate space provided for handwritten responses; and

- the functional layout to minimize gridding errors.

**4.5 If an electronic answer form for use by students is required, the following factors should be considered:**

- the layout of the electronic answer form should, if possible, be provided in a similar format to the paper answer document;

- student response areas should be clearly designated;

- the student interface should be designed in a way that helps ensure clear indication to students regarding the selections they have made;

- ability to change answers prior to submission should be provided, where applicable;

- ability to review and confirm responses recorded on the electronic answer form should be provided, where applicable; and

- the age of students who are expected to use an electronic answer form should affect the design, with special consideration paid to the age of the students as related to the requirement to interact with all aspects of the answer document.

**4.6 If an electronic answer form for use by teachers and administrators is required (when students have their answers recorded for them), the following factors should be considered:**

- the layout of the electronic answer form should, if possible, be provided in a similar format to the paper answer form;

- responses entered into the electronic answer form should be clearly indicated;

- the ability to change answers or reset the answer form prior to submission should be provided to the teacher/administrator entering student responses, where applicable; and

- the ability to review and confirm responses recorded on the electronic answer form should be provided, where applicable.

**4.7 The service provider will provide the client with all relevant psychometric information about the proposed paper-based or technology-based test forms or item pools, along with information on each iteration of changes made to the items, forms, or item pools, as set forth in the contract. The client will use this information to review and approve the test form(s) or item pool(s), keeping in mind universal design principles. This information may include:**

- average difficulty or difficulty targets of the test form or pool;

- distribution of difficulties across the form or pool;

- item and test characteristic curves;

- balance of items that may contain any DIF;

- answer key and alignment information; and

- prior parameter estimates for common items to be used in form equating, where applicable.

**4.8 The service provider will provide the client with information to use in the review and approval process, as set forth in the contract. Such information should include the following:**

- the items selected for the operational form or testing pool, along with the agreed-upon meta-data;

- the draft formatted version(s) of test booklets or the technology-based delivery format;

- the final version of test booklets or technology-based forms prior to production;

- formatted version of assessments with embedded field-test items, if applicable;

- the final version of answer documents, including demographic data collection, as defined by program requirements;

- associated paper or electronic manuals; and

- the final copy of all special test versions, which may include braille and large print, in languages other than English, audio, and scripts for read-aloud and translations.

# CHAPTER 5. STAND-ALONE FIELD TESTING

## Introduction

There are several different types of "stand-alone" preoperational testing events in common use (e.g., cognitive laboratories, pilot tests, field tests). It is best practice to conduct at least one stand-alone testing event. In instances where it is not practical or appropriate to embed test items within an operational paper-based or technology-based assessment, a separate independent "stand-alone" testing is necessary. Such instances include, for example, when student fatigue is a concern with an assessment that is already operational, or when new item types or new system functionality need to be tested prior to operational use. The goal of administering this field test is to collect performance statistics on items, performance tasks, and/or writing prompts used to inform the later selection of operational assessment items.

The decision to conduct these field tests within the client's state, outside the state, and/or with a specific cohort of students, rather than embed the field-test items within an operational form, is a result of a number of factors. Some considerations include:

- Security — writing prompts and performance tasks involve security issues because they are typically capable of being memorized;
- Timing of contract administration — there are instances when it is "too late" in a particular assessment cycle to conduct an embedded field test, or when an entirely new testing program is beginning;
- Operational attributes — administration constraints dictate the test/session length, precluding the incorporation of embedded field-test items;
- High-stakes testing — there are advantages and disadvantages of embedding field-test items in a high stakes assessment;
- Test design — testing or psychometric decisions require everyone to take the same set of items;
- New item types — there is a need to prepare students and systems (e.g., technology infrastructure, scoring capabilities) for the introduction of item types or user experiences into the program;

- Functionality — it takes time to introduce new system tools (e.g., highlighter, protractor, magnifier) and accessibility features (e.g., screen reader, assistive technology devices);
- New delivery mode — it takes time to introduce new testing modes (e.g., CAT, LOFT) and determine their impact on psychometric models; and
- Special populations — there is a need to try out items or forms/pools to see how they work with special populations.

**5.1 Field test elements should be defined and mutually agreed upon by the client and the service provider. Such elements may include:**

5.1.1 Field test specifications should be defined in such a way as to yield a balance in the required number of items needed later for operational administration, by item type and by requirements for content coverage, as defined by specifications.

5.1.2 For fixed forms, the number of field test forms and individual form layouts should be defined to produce the required yield (number of items) and to satisfy necessary administration requirements (e.g., there may need to be multiple sessions of field testing to match operational administration needs). The number of field test forms is dependent on the total number of students that can be tested. If technology-enhanced item types are being field tested, the forms cannot be delivered on paper.

5.1.3 For testing modes that are using pooled items (e.g., CAT, LOFT), the blueprint, algorithm, and item order sequence parameters should support the pool size required by the measurement model.

5.1.4 The participation guidelines should be defined and distributed as part of solicitation communications. If the field test is administered electronically, potential participants should receive the same information about hardware and software requirements as for the operational administration, as well as student practice opportunities with the delivery engine.

5.1.5    The schedule for administration, scoring, and analysis work should be created.

**5.2    Field test procedures for special populations should be agreed upon by the client and the service provider. Such procedures may include:**

5.2.1    Field tests for alternative assessment formats (e.g., braille, large print) should be conducted using only students within each targeted subgroup or special population.

5.2.2    Field testing involving special populations should occur with students receiving the appropriate paper-based or technology-based accommodations allowed for the particular assessment form used, as determined by the individual student IEP and/or 504 plan.

# CHAPTER 6. PRODUCTION OF TEST MATERIALS

## Introduction

Best practices for producing paper-based assessment materials (6.1-6.8) and for technology-based assessment materials (6.9) involve or include systems and procedures that ensure the production of appropriate material types and volumes and appropriate delivery procedures, including the need for interoperability in the delivery of materials in electronic formats. Checks and balances must be put in place to ensure that materials are properly produced, whether for technology-based or paper-based assessments, and that they facilitate efficient and accurate use by the client.

This process also must be easily replicable to account for separate accommodations materials, as well as client requests for extra materials or breach forms.

**6.1  All test materials, including files, should meet contract specifications and the service provider's processing requirements.**

    6.1.1  All materials should be controlled in a manner that ensures:

- product specifications are met;

- technical specifications for form, fit, and function are achieved;

- quality acceptance criteria are achieved;

- traceability and record retention are maintained; and

- conformity with established security policies (see Chapters 8 and 11).

    6.1.2  Materials critical to the successful capture and scoring of the assessment program should be controlled for, including:

- correct stock;

- correct ink;

- scanning indicators, where applicable;

- completeness and accuracy; and

- storage and handling requirements.

6.2 A process should be established and approved by the service provider and the client to help ensure production of necessary quantities of manufactured materials, based upon enrollment data and overage requirements provided by the client.

    6.2.1 This process should include a way to estimate the materials required at the testing sites and could include developing an algorithm for estimating the overall quantity of materials needed.

    6.2.2 Information to begin this process may come from student enrollment and participation databases (see 18.2.2); therefore, the client and the service provider should establish and implement a process for maximizing the interoperability of those systems that share such data.

    6.2.3 A specifications document that includes a materials list should be developed. This document should delineate all of the material requirements, including a plan for additional orders of materials that may be requested.

    6.2.4 A document containing specific quantities for all materials, including recommended overage and special forms (i.e., braille, large print, forms in languages other than English, and other special materials), should be produced.

6.3 A process should be established to help ensure that all test materials meet specifications prior to final production. The quality assurance process should include checks during file production, media replication, duplication and packaging, and/or printing.

6.4 A process should be established to help ensure accurate collating of test materials. The collating process should include a page-signature verification system or similar system, which could employ bar code readers, and/or operator checklists, and/or spot checks.

6.5 A process should be established to identify and manage secure materials (see Chapter 8).

6.5.1 A specifications document should be created that defines security requirements, such as the placement of a unique security code, size, configuration, and read requirements, as delineated in other sections of this document.

6.5.2 For electronic materials, specifications may include storage (including all back-ups), encryption of files, unique identifiers for distributed files, etc.

6.5.3 A process should be established to account for and replace secure materials that may be damaged as a part of the production process.

6.5.4 A process should be established to account for and manage secure materials that are to be kept onsite for extended periods of time.

6.5.5 A process and timeline should be established for destruction of overage materials and electronic files that are no longer needed.

**6.6 A process should be established, where required, to precode answer documents with state-assigned unique student identification and demographic information, LEA and school/testing site codes, etc. Alternately, this process should establish unique testing sessions for students identified in advance of testing, or establish a specified quantity of testing sessions (see further discussion in Chapter 18).**

6.6.1 The service provider should work closely with the client to define required data elements and to determine schedules and procedures for the transfer of electronic precoded data, including an evaluation of interoperability standards for use in sharing all such data and implementation of a process for maximizing interoperability.

6.6.2 The client should provide an electronic data file that contains the most current student identification, demographic, and available score attribution information to allow for the accurate administration, scoring, and reporting of standardized tests at identified points in time.

6.6.3 The service provider should work closely with the client to define a process to manage changes to the precoded data file.

6.6.4 Human-readable information should be included on the barcode label or preprinted on the answer document. This should provide enough information to match the answer document to the appropriate student.

6.6.5 A unique barcode should be printed on the answer document, which will link to the electronic student data file.

**6.7 A process should be established to ensure all materials, including accommodations and breach materials, are spiraled, if necessary, and then shrink-wrapped, banded, or packaged according to the contract specifications.**

6.7.1 The spiraling process should include quality checks to help ensure accuracy, and could employ:

- bar code readers; and/or

- operator checklists.

6.7.2 Shrink-wrapped or banded packages should have clear identification of contents. This should be completed by using:

- example range sheets;

- visible first and last documents; and

- content description labels.

6.7.3 A process should be determined for production of additional materials, if needed, including production of breach forms and associated materials.

6.7.4 The plan and timeline for production of additional materials should be developed and agreed upon by the client and the service provider.

**6.8 A process should be established to ensure selection of appropriate technology-based media to support file size and test administration (e.g., server-based systems, CDs, DVDs, USB flash drives).**

6.8.1   All materials should be controlled in a manner that ensures technical specifications for form, fit, and function are achieved, including file format and display resolution.

6.8.2   If the test will be administered using external media, there should be a process for assembling the various elements of a test package electronically, using custom software applications, duplication, replication, and packaging of test files on appropriate media (e.g., CDs, DVDs, USB flash drives). This process should include a way to estimate the materials required at the testing site and could include developing an algorithm for estimating the overall quantity of materials needed.

**6.9   Procedures should be developed, documented, and implemented to handle assessment delivery and delivery system interoperability.**

6.9.1   The client and the service provider should evaluate available interoperability standards regarding the grouping or arrangement of items in test forms or item pools. The data structures of the standard should be flexible enough to address the needs of the assessment design (e.g., fixed form linear and/or adaptive forms) and should provide information on how items are scored, weighted, or grouped for scoring purposes. If the test is adaptive, identification of the algorithm used, and any parameters necessary for the algorithm to operate, should be supported.

6.9.2   In defining test delivery and scoring interoperability, the client and the service provider should address the following areas:

6.9.2.1   Form and pool definitions. Establish and document procedures to ensure that the standardized test form or item pool defines all information necessary to deliver, score, and report the results of a test, including but not limited to:

- content elements, tools, and ancillary material or information (e.g., instructions) that must be presented to the student;

- on what platforms the form or item pool is designed for delivery;

- how the items and materials are to be sequenced (e.g., fixed form item order, CAT algorithm parameters);

- if and when the student can review or change answers;

- what accessibility features are available in the test; and

- timing requirements.

6.9.2.2 Multiple platform presentations. Establish and document procedures to enable consistent and interoperable test presentation, which should include the following:

- test presentation information should be provided separately from the test definition, in order to allow for the test to be used on multiple delivery platforms;

- test presentation information should build upon the item presentation information and include nonitem structures, as appropriate; for example, in a paper-based administration, instructions, page headers and footers, and section breaks (e.g., stop sign pages), must be structured;

- navigation controls and tools (calculators, rulers, etc.) for technology-based assessments must be supported across platforms; and

- test presentation structures may include templates, style guides, etc., and/or strategies for providing platform specific presentation and layout.

6.9.2.3 Monitoring and evaluating new developments in content delivery so that interoperability can be considered as new delivery systems become available.

**6.10 Quality assurance (QA) procedures should be established and implemented to ensure produced materials conform to the specifications. These procedures should be completed, and the adherence to specifications confirmed, prior to sign-off of product for distribution.**

6.10.1 The QA plan for both paper-based and technology-based assessments should include, but not be limited to, elements, such as the agreed upon level of quality, expected sampling frequency, a final inspection plan, and acceptance criteria.

6.10.2 The plan should address notification to the client in the event of any QA finding and proposed resolution.

**6.11 The QA plan should include in-process quality control checks.**

6.11.1 A QA plan for paper-based assessment should identify the appropriate points in the production process for quality control checks, the sampling frequency of in-process materials, and the retention policy for those samples.

6.11.2 In addition to the in-process checks for paper-based assessments, a QA plan for technology-based assessments should also include checks for file integrity during the file master and replication process (if produced on physical media).

**6.12 The QA plan for technology-based assessments should be developed and implemented to assure the assessment will work as specified in the operational testing environment.**

6.12.1 In-process checks should be identified and conducted to assure that specifications are being met as the assessment is being produced.

6.12.2    An end-to-end assessment validation should be conducted to ensure that all components of the assessment perform as expected (e.g., performance speed, item presentation, item resolution, and other functions as specified).

6.12.3    The end-to-end assessment validation should be conducted on systems that mirror the systems and materials that students will be using.

# CHAPTER 7. THIRD-PARTY MANAGEMENT

## Introduction

Service providers often engage outside parties to fulfill component projects of a statewide testing program. These third-party subcontractors can be vendors, software development organizations, hardware and Internet providers, application service providers, service centers, freelancers, or consultants who may or may not be named in a service provider's proposal. In all instances, management best practices will apply to the service provider and all such third parties to ensure adherence to contractual obligations; however, the service provider is ultimately responsible for the deliverables from the third party. Additionally, service providers should be required to name any third-party providers who will be responsible for writing or maintaining any portion of the code base for a technology-based assessment delivery system or for handling secure electronic content or data. The exact detail and level of responsibility should be specified in work-related documents.

7.1   **The client may establish requirements for the use of third-party providers consistent with applicable procurement laws (see Chapter 20). Specific requirements may include the use of in-state providers, minority-owned businesses, women-owned businesses, and major subcontractors added after the contract is awarded.**

7.2   **A third party may or may not be named in the service provider's proposal to the client.**

   7.2.1   When a third party is named, it should be designated as a subcontractor with responsibility for specific project work or service to be delivered.

   7.2.2   Unnamed third parties providing services are typically vendors, freelancers, or consultants. These third-party providers usually provide a commoditized or customized service and it is the service provider's responsibility to ensure these entities adhere to the contract.

7.3   The service provider has a responsibility to the client to ensure that the third party (named or unnamed) delivers on the agreed-upon requirements. In order to help ensure that the contractual obligations are met, the service provider should:

- establish confidentiality agreements, data access and protection protocols, and nondisclosure agreements;

- ensure preparation of contracts for services and necessary work orders;

- define the scope of work to be delivered by the third party;

- agree on, document, and institute a Service Level Agreement (SLA), that includes the scope of work, quality expectations, and turnaround of services (see 15.8);

- define program management expectations; and

- establish communication and escalation protocols.

7.4   The third party has a responsibility directly to the service provider and indirectly to the client through the service provider. The third-party provider should:

- provide a letter of commitment, if named as a subcontractor or if required by the client;

- designate a project manager or other point-of-contact person responsible for third-party deliverables; and

- establish licensing arrangements for any intellectual property or other assets owned by the third party, consistent with requested requirements and obligations (e.g., software incorporated into the client solution).

# CHAPTER 8. SECURITY

## Introduction

The integrity of state test results, as well as the fairness and validity of inferences or decisions based on those results, are dependent upon maintaining the security of the items and tests, as well as the answer documents and certain ancillary materials that result from test administrations. Moreover, test security also involves making sure that the client and the service provider adopt and adhere to a written security plan, and any associated policies and procedures that minimize the risks of test theft and cheating, internally and externally, not only by students, but also by adults who can negatively affect the integrity of the testing program. This chapter discusses best practices for achieving test security throughout the assessment process of all paper-based and technology-based assessments, using methods that support the accessibility needs of students with disabilities and English learners. The cooperation of the service provider (and any subcontractors) and the client is essential, as are the efforts of the teachers, supervisors, administrators, and others at district and school sites, who receive and distribute test materials, administer and monitor student testing, and return test materials for scoring and reporting. The overall effectiveness of the effort requires careful planning and communication.

The success of security efforts depends on an understanding of the security threats to statewide large-scale assessments. Specific threats can be seen in the typical security breaches encountered by state programs, including some breaches that are similar to those experienced by non-educational assessment programs. Typical breaches include:

1.  Gaining unauthorized access to secure test materials by students, school officials, teachers, proctors, and/or principals, at any time in the assessment process, except when specifically required for the proper administration of the assessments;

2.  Unauthorized copying, reproducing, or sharing all, or any portion of, test materials;

3.  Providing inappropriate assistance to students (e.g., direct or indirect coaching of students, anything altering the standardized administration procedures, making answers available, or changing answers); and

4.  Gaining unauthorized access to answer sheets, test results, or scoring databases by students, school officials, teachers, proctors, and/or principals, in order to change answers, scores, or results.

This chapter addresses various security measures that seek to reduce the likelihood of potential breaches or to deal directly with breaches that occur through the testing process, including:

*   development and implementation of comprehensive security plans for both the service provider and the client, including coverage of paper-based and technology-based assessments and protection of all related data, including test results (physical reports and databases);
*   development and implementation of security training and related material for all personnel involved in the testing process, including proctors, teachers, principals, and test administrators;
*   use of security, confidentiality, and nondisclosure agreements;
*   detection and handling of security breaches occurring at any point during the testing process;
*   defining and implementing security for administration of both paper-based and technology-based assessments, including mixed-mode testing;
*   protection of test materials before, during, and after test administration; and
*   protection of student test records and other sensitive personal student data.

8.1 **The service provider will develop and implement a security plan covering its internal processes (e.g., item development, pilot or field testing, test construction, materials production and distribution, scoring, data processing and analyses, and reporting).**

8.1.1 The service provider should submit a copy of its existing internal security plan to the client for consideration during service provider selection and contract negotiations.

8.1.2 Following selection, the client may offer recommendations for changes in the service provider's internal security procedures and the service provider shall consider those recommendations and provide a response to the client.

8.2 **A comprehensive plan to provide security of intellectual property (owned by the client or others), as well as of paper or electronic data (e.g., demographic data, school/teacher/student information, and assessment results), will be developed, agreed upon, and implemented by the client in collaboration with the service provider. The plan should identify the means to prevent potential breaches in security. In addition, the plan should specify the roles and responsibilities, including procedures, when any party has control over secure tests and related materials.**

8.2.1 The security plan should establish, document, and implement rules for storage and access of secure materials, whether paper or electronic, in all facilities under the client's control (e.g., offices, warehouses), as well as storage and access in schools and other local facilities not under the control of the client, but with whom the client communicates or distributes test materials and secure data (e.g., student data, test results, and score reports).

8.2.2 The plan should establish and document procedures and rules for the security of test materials, whether paper or electronic, when they are under joint control during item development, test construction, materials production, test distribution, and processing, including rules for:

- storage of and access to items, tests, and test results, whether in physical documents (e.g., check-in and check-out procedures) or in electronic databases and reporting systems;

- item review meetings, standard setting activities, and other instances where access to operational items is necessary; and

- secure materials retrieval and destruction.

8.2.3   To the extent that the primary service provider uses third parties in providing services to the client, the plan should provide guidance to the primary service provider that covers maintenance of security at subcontractor or vendor sites. This plan should include rules for the following:

- training and sharing training materials;

- securing materials during the transfer (through physical or electronic means) between a third party and the service provider, and the transfer between a third party and the client;

- securing materials during any contracted services (e.g., item writing, scoring);

- storage of and access to test materials and test results, whether in physical documents or databases and reporting systems, if they are housed, stored, or hosted at the third party's site(s);

- retrieval or disposition (i.e., deletion and/or destruction) of secure materials at the third party's site(s); and

- obtaining and managing security, nondisclosure, or confidentiality agreements for all personnel who will have access to secure materials.

8.2.4   The plan should establish and document procedures and rules to secure all computer systems related to the state program, including managing access to Internet connectivity on computers used for test development activities, delivery of assessments, or exchanging or accessing data and information, whether such connectivity is required at the facilities of the client, the service provider, or a third party. Areas for attention will include the following:

- system access should be protected by the use of passwords and/or PINs so that information is only available to personnel who have been authorized for such access, which may be different than an individual's access to the facility where the computer system exists (see 8.2.6);

- the process in control of the system access should also monitor and record all accesses and attempts to gain access (e.g., using physical logs or electronic recordkeeping);

- computers or other Net-centric devices, and assistive technologies, used for administration of assessments must not allow students to have unauthorized access to the Internet during test administration, or in the case of actual online assessments, such connectivity must be protected by adequate methods; and

- appropriate protections (e.g., spam filters, firewalls, anti-virus software, anti-malware software) should be installed on computers used for accessing student results and other sensitive/confidential data, and appropriate procedures established and implemented to update security, including installation of software patches.

8.2.5 The plan should identify a method to secure electronic transfer of test materials and information (e.g., use of industry standard encryption methods for data exchange). The plan should establish procedures to make and keep facilities secure. These procedures should include the use of:

- identification badges or electronic access/identity cards for all employees and guests;

- visitor policy regulations;

- security access systems (e.g., locked rooms, coded or card entry systems), especially for secure offices within a facility that is not itself secure; and

- levels of security and access controls appropriate for the circumstances, type of facility and computer system, and level of responsibility (i.e., how much the individual staff person needs to know).

8.2.6    The plan should establish procedures and rules for the secure administration of the assessment. These procedures should include the use of:

- authentication of students (e.g., visual recognition, checking school photo ID's, student ID numbers, use of computer ID's and passwords) and comprehensive monitoring during test administration; and

- security practices that conform to all of the requirements for standardized test administration contained in 8.8.

8.2.7    The plan should establish procedures and policies to carry out an item release process, if any, as well as other legislated or legal aspects of the client program requirements that might appear to be in conflict with otherwise appropriate test security. The client should work with the service provider to maximize the security of all test materials, including secure test content.

8.2.8    The client and the service provider should undertake periodic audits of their respective security plans, so that problems with any procedures can be documented and reported to the other, and so that appropriate steps can be taken to modify the plan. The results of such audits should be contained in written reports. The client should establish with the service provider when and how widely such reports will be circulated, including whether they will be communicated to stakeholders and the media.

8.2.9  The plan should establish procedures and rules for the monitoring and investigating of personnel who have signed security agreements (see 8.3), or who are part of the test administration process in the districts and schools (e.g., teachers, principals, test administrators), to ensure that they comply and carry out their roles in the testing process. Such procedures should cover:

- prevention of improper use of, or failure to use, security procedures, including obtaining or seeking to obtain inappropriate access to secure facilities and/or computer systems, failing to follow established procedures for administration of secure tests, lack of protection of test scores, or inappropriate access to test score reports or databases;

- use of appropriate detection methods (see 8.12) to determine if personnel have violated security procedures, including, but not limited to, providing test content, answers and/or assistance to students prior to and/or during test administration, or inappropriately accessing paper-based or technology-based assessments or student databases containing tests or scores; and

- notification and education of affected personnel in order to ensure they are aware of the procedures and rules that will be implemented, as well as the potential consequences that may be imposed for violation of those procedures and rules, and the due process rules for resolving such violations (see 8.8.2).

8.2.10  The plan should establish and implement procedures and rules governing how and when the client will provide the service provider with the necessary secure information on each student to be assessed, including sufficient information about the district, school, and class for which a test administration is scheduled, as well as procedures for protecting and using those data as part of the security scheme around planning for test administration.

8.3 **Procedures should be established and implemented to handle selection and responsibilities of all personnel who have access to secure materials.**

    8.3.1    Security, nondisclosure, and confidentiality agreements, or similar legal documents requiring that test materials must be secured and protected from unauthorized copying, reproducing, sharing, or any other type of disclosure, should be required for personnel of the client, the service provider, or the third-party subcontractor who are to have access to secure test materials and/or confidential and secure data.

    8.3.2    Where appropriate, procedures and rules should be established and implemented to obtain security background checks on all personnel who will have access to secure materials or secure databases.

8.4 **Training materials regarding security should be developed and training conducted on security topics.**

    8.4.1    Training materials for all aspects of security specific to each person's role in the assessment program should be developed, with input from the service provider and the client. Such training materials should be:

- based upon, and consistent with, the security plan (see 8.2);

- specifically oriented to whether the assessment program is paper-based, technology-based, or mixed mode;

- designed to educate and inform staff of the client, the service provider (and any third parties), and district and school personnel who have a role in the client's testing program, including how to ensure that test security is maintained while providing needed access to individuals with disabilities and English learners;

- designed to explain the consequences of noncompliance with the security plan and the specific procedures for notification, retraining, and monitoring protocols; and

- maintained and updated to provide current information and procedures.

8.4.2   Procedures for training all necessary personnel of the client, the service provider, and subcontractor in security measures, including the overall importance of security, should be documented and implemented. Such training should be available through scheduled or on-demand sessions to reach all necessary personnel.

8.4.3   A communications plan should be developed to ensure that all stakeholders in the assessment are informed about the training that is required and when and how it is available.

## 8.5   Policies and procedures for preventing and dealing with possible security breaches should be developed and implemented.

8.5.1   Procedures, including contingency plans, should be in place to handle all likely breaches in security. These procedures should include the following:

- specifying what constitutes different types of security breaches and appropriate methods for dealing with them;

- replacement of existing test forms with a breach form;

- replacement of specific compromised items in an existing form;

- scoring and re-scoring ability with the exclusion of specific items from scoring;

- conducting an investigation into the causes of the breach, which may include forensic analyses (see 8.12);

- provisions regarding due process and consequences for students (e.g., invalidation of scores, retesting); and

- provisions regarding due process and consequences for teachers, principals, and other school officials.

8.5.2 Procedures should include a recovery plan for any type of database security breach, including the steps that should be taken if a breach should occur.

8.5.3 Procedures should include a plan for responding to a security breach that jeopardizes, potentially jeopardizes, or invalidates student test score results, including the use of any of the options identified above.

8.5.4 If the breach procedure necessitates the use of a breach test form, the development of that form, or multiple forms, should be coordinated with all program needs and requirements.

8.5.5 A communications plan should be developed and implemented so that all identified stakeholders in the assessment program are informed and educated about what steps should be taken if a breach occurs. The communications plan should also identify a strategy for when and how information on security breaches is disseminated to stakeholders, the media, and the general public.

**8.6 Procedures and rules should be established and implemented to secure items, item pools, and associated meta-data, during periods of item development. The procedures should be designed to protect the integrity of the assessment program and to discourage cheating, and should address the following:**

8.6.1 Securing test items during the entire development process, including uses of innovative item types and test forms.

8.6.2 The secure transfer of either digital or paper formats of test items and related test materials from one development location to another, and from one individual or device to another (see 8.2.5).

8.6.3 Ensuring that personnel who are involved in authoring or reviewing items are hired, selected, and assigned responsibilities using appropriate methods (see 8.4). Personnel should have access assigned to secure information and materials based on their responsibilities.

8.6.4 The use of computer systems to author or review items and other test materials, including using appropriate access security (see 8.2.4).

8.6.5 Providing item security during item revision, including documentation of each user and changes made.

8.6.6 Disposal of secure documents and digital files upon completion of their use during the item development process (see 8.9).

**8.7 Procedures should be developed and implemented to account for and protect secure materials, including test items, forms and other materials (e.g., graphic files, answers sheets, scoring rubrics, including for electronic student responses for hand or automated scoring of technology-based assessments) in both paper and digital formats, at all stages of distribution, receipt, storage, and return.**

8.7.1 These procedures should address how security issues will be managed at state and local levels, for materials in all formats.

8.7.2 The service provider and the client must ensure that secure materials are accounted for as they are packaged, distributed, received, stored, and eventually returned to the service provider, including use of a documented chain of custody process for tracking all secure materials. The security procedures for each of these steps are discussed in more detail in Chapters 10, 11, 12, and 18. Characteristics of a security system, whether it is for paper-based or technology-based assessments, may include:

- unique student ID numbers;

- unique document ID numbers;

- bar code labels (paper-based tests only);

- unique security ID numbers;

- digital versions of secure materials should be encrypted during distribution, using an accepted encryption standard;

- digital materials should be stored in an encrypted form for the shortest amount of time necessary before test administration;

- when secure materials are stored locally (e.g., in the district and school), access by local personnel should be strictly limited and access should only be in accordance with appropriate security measures for facilities and computer systems (see 8.2.4 and 8.2.7); and

- the same security procedures should be used for breach forms as are used for the original test forms.

8.7.3 All distributed materials should have a known and documented destination (e.g., warehouse, school, host IP address). Receipt or acknowledgement procedures should be established and documented. These procedures should address the following:

- reconciling the expected quantity to be received with the actual quantity of documents received;

- maintaining a log of received and returned materials;

- using secure, traceable tracking methods; and

- developing a chain of custody procedure (see chapter 11) and a reconciliation procedure (to include a final accounting of materials), which may involve counting materials received and/or scanning receipts.

**8.8 Procedures and rules for test administration, including the monitoring of students and the management of possible testing irregularities, should be developed, implemented and communicated to all necessary parties, including for the following:**

8.8.1 Secure administration, with training provided to the appropriate individuals (see Chapter 9). At a minimum, these procedures and training should address the following:

- proper handling of secure materials;

- secure storage of materials prior to, during, and after administration, as detailed elsewhere in this chapter (see 8.2.4 and 8.7.2);

- authenticating students;

- using test administration schedules, including arranging test sessions by content area, and breaks;

- monitoring or proctoring students during the test, between test sessions, and during unscheduled breaks;

- arranging test administration rooms (for both paper-based and technology-based assessments) and following the necessary security procedures for test administration (e.g., for paper-based tests, using different test forms so that students sitting next to each other do not have identical test booklets; for technology-based assessments, arranging work stations so that students cannot see another student's computer screen);

- proper handling of tests given with accommodations and/or in alternative assessment formats (e.g., advance preparation of hardware/software, testing in separate rooms, across multiple days, or using allowable accommodations); and

- obtaining signed nondisclosure, confidentiality, or security agreements/oaths from test administrators, proctors, and any others who have access to secure materials, or who monitor students during the test administration.

8.8.2    Prevention and/or response to instances of testing irregularities and cheating, including the following:

- training of teachers, proctors, and district and school administrators;

- preparation of testing irregularity reports, including how to return those reports to the proper authority;

- immediately handling security problems during the student authentication process and/or problems during test administration;

- providing an explanation to both students and test administrators/proctors of consequences of testing irregularities and cheating; and

- establishing guidance for proctors, teachers, and school officials, as well as due process requirements, where appropriate.

8.8.3   Authenticating students, acceptable methods for which may include one or more of the following:

- verification of student identity upon entry into the school or classroom, by school official or teacher, based upon visual recognition or display of valid form(s) of identification;

- comparison of student roster against those present at the test administration;

- use of seating charts during the test administration; and

- reliance on electronic monitoring of each computer workstation.

8.8.4   Handling secure test materials, including answer sheets with student answers, by teachers, principals, and other school officials before returning them to the service provider, including the following:

- to the extent feasible, teachers or instructors should not be assigned as test administrators or proctors for their own students; in the event that teachers or instructors proctor their own students, they should be reminded of security ramifications and appropriate procedures (see 9.5.4 for rules and responsibilities of administrators and proctors);

- to the extent feasible, teachers, proctors, and school officials should not have access and opportunity to change individual student test answers (paper-based or technology-based), during or after test administration, including access to change scores in test databases and reports; and

- computer systems should not allow changes in student test answers after the session is completed (e.g., session times out, test is submitted).

**8.9  Procedures should be established and implemented to account for and protect secure materials following test administration.**

8.9.1  Procedures for the return of all secure materials should be documented and communicated to appropriate individuals for implementation. The procedures should address the actions and any consequences associated with missing or altered materials.

8.9.2  Procedures for disposition and salvage of secure materials should be established and implemented. These procedures should include:

- authorizing appropriate individuals to delete or destroy materials;

- establishing a process for when and how secure materials will be disposed of or archived;

- establishing a process for proper handling of returned materials; and

- certification or verification that secure materials were deleted or destroyed.

**8.10  Procedures and rules should be established and implemented to assure appropriate scoring of test results, which should address:**

8.10.1  Protecting the integrity of the scoring process for all item types, including monitoring and evaluating the scoring process to avoid opportunities to change inappropriately any responses or scores.

8.10.2 Participation of teachers, test administrators, principals, and other school officials in the scoring process.

8.10.3 Use of outside personnel to score test responses, including procedures to transfer secure test materials in "read only" formats.

8.10.4 Protecting test results once scores have been recorded and stored in scoring databases, including restricting access to such databases to authorized individuals (see 8.2.4 and 8.2.6).

**8.11 Procedures and rules should be established and implemented to protect the integrity of the statewide assessment process when assessments are used at multiple locations (e.g., across the state or in multiple states).**

8.11.1 When a test administration window lasts longer than a few hours, especially if there are time zone differences, that makes it possible for items and answers to be disclosed to students who have not yet taken the test, the client and the service provider should take steps to protect against disclosures, including consulting with other states that may be administering the same assessment (e.g., in a consortium situation).

8.11.2 No one, including students, teachers, proctors and other school officials, should be able to copy, reproduce or obtain a copy of test items (paper-based or technology-based) during or after the test administration window within the state or states conducting the same assessment.

8.11.3 The client and the service provider should establish procedures to monitor the Internet and social websites before, during, and after test administration for any evidence that items and/or answers to completed tests have been shared (i.e., shared directly online or shared offline but the evidence is available online).

8.11.4 Procedures should be established to remove or block such postings that threaten the security and integrity of the statewide assessment program, where feasible.

8.11.5  Procedures should be established to take appropriate steps, including legal action, if necessary, against persons who violate security policies.

**8.12  The plan should include procedures for detecting irregularities in student test scores. Among the available forensic methods that may be used are:**

8.12.1  Erasure analyses to analyze and uncover if paper answer sheets have been altered inappropriately by students, teachers or school officials (paper-based tests only). Erasure analyses should include:

- wrong-to-wrong answer changes;

- wrong-to-right answer changes;

- right-to-wrong answer changes; and

- comparison of percentage of wrong-to-right answer changes to all erasures on the answer form.

8.12.2  Collusion/similarity analyses to analyze unusual patterns of similarity among test results and determine if, and to what extent, collusion among students, test administrators, teachers, or school officials occurred.

8.12.3  Aberrance analyses to indicate the existence of unusual test response patterns for individual results, which may indicate cheating or test theft activities, or simply that the test responses do not represent an appropriate or trustworthy set of responses to items.

8.12.4  Technology-based assessments provide other response data to be used for forensic analyses. These types of analyses may include response time data, keystroke patterns (e.g., typed responses to essays), multiple responses, orders of items, and response changes history.

**8.13  Procedures for secure storage of test materials and results should be established and implemented.**

8.13.1  Procedures and policies should be established for the short-term and long-term storage of secure test materials, test results, and any security-related reports or analyses.

8.13.2 Procedures and policies should be established for the appropriate disclosure, including disclosure for legal purposes, and use of archived test content and test results.

8.13.3 Physical test materials, such as test booklets, answer sheets, and other secure materials, should be stored and protected against attack or disaster in a secure environment, with access only by authorized individuals (for paper-based assessments only).

8.13.4 Digital test materials should be stored securely and accessed only by authorized individuals.

8.13.5 Backup and disaster recovery policies and procedures should be established for materials.

8.13.6 Procedures should be established and implemented to assure protection of all intellectual property, whether owned by the client or the service provider, and the privacy of student identifiable information and related student test data, including compliance with the Family Educational Rights and Privacy Act (FERPA) and any state laws and regulations governing privacy or access to records (e.g., student record laws, public record laws).

8.14 The client and the service provider should establish procedures and rules to ensure compliance with state and local laws, regulations, and policies for the protection of students (e.g., background checks, finger-printing, visitor log).

# CHAPTER 9. TEST ADMINISTRATION

## Introduction

This chapter highlights the best practices for administration of assessments—whether paper-based, technology-based or mixed mode. The client and the service provider should collaborate to establish the most efficient and secure test administration practices feasible, while maintaining the standardization necessary across the state. After each administration, lessons learned should be reviewed and refinements, with appropriate planning, should be integrated into the next administration cycle.

9.1 **An annual calendar for the administration of all assessments, whether paper-based, technology-based, and/or mixed-mode systems, should be identified and published well in advance, which may be done for multiple years at one time, when practical.**

   9.1.1 The test administration calendar should be available on the client's website and publicly announced at the time of posting.

   9.1.2 The final, approved calendar should not be altered or revised unless conditions make it absolutely necessary.

   9.1.3 If calendar changes are necessary, they should be negotiated with the service provider (and other impacted stakeholders), announced, and version control implemented.

9.2 **The testing schedule, by administration mode, should articulate which days each assessment will be administered and how much time will be allocated to each assessment. In addition, adjustments in the testing schedule or in test administration procedures will be made for students needing more time, accommodations, and untimed assessments, where applicable (see Chapter 19). Available resources for technology-based assessments must be considered when creating the testing schedule and in establishing pre-administration technical support requirements (see Chapter 15).**

9.2.1 If appropriate, a timing study should be conducted to validate the time needed to administer a new test.

9.2.2 Time necessary for administration of each mode should include the following activities, related to administration schedule, as appropriate:

- test administrator preparation prior to student engagement;

- student engagement of the test, including instructions, sample items, and/or practice tests;

- test administrator close-out of administration session(s);

- use of multiple test segments during a single administration session;

- use of appropriate accommodations under the conditions documented in Chapter 19; and

- student breaks.

**9.3 Coordination of a statewide assessment requires specific roles to be defined at the state, district, and school levels.**

9.3.1 Districts should designate a district assessment and technology coordinator for all communications and coordination of the state assessment.

9.3.2 Schools should designate a building assessment coordinator for all communications and coordination of the state assessment.

9.3.3 Contact lists of coordinators and administrators with all pertinent contact information should be maintained and used. These lists should include state, district, and building contacts (e.g. support and escalation procedures).

**9.4 The service provider and the client should develop student-level directions that specify the exact instructions to be presented to students in written or oral form. They should also agree on how and when student-level directions for administration of each test mode should be made available prior to the administration window.**

9.4.1 Scripted directions for students must make clear what is to be written or orally presented by the test administrator and what the procedural directions should be for the test administrator.

    9.4.1.1 Scripted directions for students should be written specifically for each grade level, content area, and mode of delivery.

    9.4.1.2 Scripted directions for students should include instructions and/or provisions for different administration configurations for the assessment (e.g., multiple segments on a single day, individual segments on separate days).

    9.4.1.3 Individuals who are not familiar with the program should review scripted student directions, as long as the scripts do not include secure materials. This will help to ensure clarity and accuracy.

9.4.2 The client and the service provider should agree upon how much time is sufficient prior to administration for delivery of materials, whether in paper or digital format. When directions contain secure material (i.e., assessment items), different delivery dates or special physical security procedures may be required for packaging paper-based assessments or delivery/storage of technology-based assessments.

9.4.3 Maintenance of security of such materials must be documented.

9.4.4 Nonsecure manuals and directions should be available (e.g., posted to a website).

9.4.5 Tutorial and practice materials should be available (e.g., distributed, posted to a website), so that students are comfortable with all aspects of the test-taking process, whether the test is delivered on paper or by technology.

**9.5 The protocol for preparing the testing environment will be outlined as a part of the procedure manuals and training.**

9.5.1 The test administrator-to-student ratio for each testing mode should be identified, either as a requirement or recommendation.

9.5.2 Administration locations and their requirements, such as allowable accommodations and appropriate seat spacing, should be identified, as determined by mode of delivery.

9.5.3 Allowable and expressly prohibited materials for student use during administration should be identified (e.g., scratch paper and calculator are allowed, but unapproved mobile devices are not). For technology-based tests some of these materials may be available in digital form, which may require special rules and administration training.

9.5.4 Roles, responsibilities, and requirements and training for assessment proctors should be defined and implemented per state policy or guidelines. Clients should consider the use of confidentiality or nondisclosure agreements as discussed in Chapter 8.

**9.6 The service provider and the client will decide when and what materials and procedures, required for training and for administration of the assessment, are made available in advance of the administration window.**

9.6.1 Such materials and procedures may include in-person or web-based training workshops.

9.6.2 The client and the service provider should agree upon the nature and focus of audiences for the test coordinator material.

- Many states publish a manual of general procedures for wide audiences, covering the administration of assessments, whether paper-based, technology-based or mixed-mode, that provides guidance on topics, such as the following:

    - an overview of the assessment program in the state, including state laws and regulations;

    - ethical practices for test administration;

- roles and responsibilities of district and school staff during the testing process;

- a process for determining and using accommodations for qualifying students and a process for challenging these determinations;

- participation requirements for students in the assessment program, including those in unique circumstances (e.g., hospitalized students);

- general administration guidance, such as scheduling and documentation;

- provision of accurate student information and demographics;

- reports available following the administration;

- necessary forms used within the assessment program; and

- information on policies for score appeals, security breaches, testing irregularities, or public review of assessments.

- Many states publish administration manuals that are specific to a particular assessment, whether it is paper-based or technology-based, and are geared to district and school administrator use during the time of an administration. These manuals may include the following information:

  - general information about particular assessments, including websites and customer service contacts;

  - procedures for administering a general assessment with allowable accommodations, alternative assessment forms, and/or alternate assessments, to special populations, including information on the state accommodation policy and allowable accommodations for each assessment (see Chapter 19);

- procedures for ordering or delivering additional materials;

- procedures for preparation of testing sites;

- procedures for maintaining secure distribution and delivery of test and support materials, whether paper-based or technology-based;

- procedures for maintaining a secure inventory of returned or stored test materials for paper-based assessments;

- procedures for physically or digitally storing and/or returning test materials to the service provider; and

- description of paper-based and/or technology-based forms used during the administration.

9.6.3 Training protocols for test administrators may be based on each test administration mode and should be standardized across the state. Training protocols and materials should specify:

• the frequency, length, and delivery mode of training sessions;

• the agenda and objectives for training;

• the procedures for conducting training with test administrators (e.g., a mock administration, using the roles of administrators, teachers/proctors, and students); and

• the procedures of verification of training and handling of verification records.

9.6.4 At the end of training, test administrators should be familiar with, at a minimum:

• the administration plan for the assessment (e.g., multiple segments on particular days);

- procedures for administering the assessment under normal standardized conditions, including delivering scripted instructions;

- procedures for reporting and correcting flaws in the test materials;

- procedures for handling technology-based assessment issues including:

  - missing or invalid credentials;

  - interruption of the testing session due to technology; and

  - definition of, and actions for, all error codes;

- procedures for reporting testing irregularities and security breaches;

- procedures for dealing with cases involving suspected cheating between students and/or teachers/administrators;

- assessment procedures when unique circumstances arise (e.g., fire alarms, power failures, severe weather alerts, student illness during administration);

- procedures for including diverse student populations;

- protocol for answering student questions about the assessment;

- procedures for handling allowable accommodations for any assessment, including any alternative assessment forms, or for the use of alternate assessments consistent with the practices described in Chapter 19;

- procedures for ensuring test security during all stages of administration, including on-site physical or digital storage, pursuant to the security practices set forth in Chapter 8; and

- procedures for allowable student activities after completing the assessment, if other students are still engaged in the assessment.

# CHAPTER 10. MATERIALS PACKAGING FOR PAPER-BASED TESTS

## Introduction

Best practices for packaging all client materials, including secure and ancillary materials, require systems and procedures designed to ensure accuracy and efficiency in both order creation and fulfillment. The ability to expedite these processes is also important, as well as the creation of accessible documentation to assist in problem resolution.

For this phase of the overall development process, it is essential that materials be organized in the most intuitive manner possible, and adequate documentation be provided, in order to facilitate efficient and accurate receipt and tracking of all materials.

**10.1 Procedures should be developed and implemented to ensure the accurate and timely packaging and delivery of orders, including additional material orders.**

10.1.1 A process should be established to specify, collect, and confirm material orders. This process should be standardized, documented, and communicated to all parties required to place orders for material distribution.

10.1.2 If training is needed for the materials order process (e.g., due to an online materials order process), training materials and scheduled training sessions should be developed and implemented for all appropriate parties.

10.1.3 A process should be established to create packing lists based upon supplied requirements. Information in the packing lists should include (at a minimum) designation of standard assessment versions, designation of accommodated assessment versions, ancillary testing materials, material quantities, and material destinations. The process should be documented and agreed upon by the client and the service provider.

10.1.4 Procedures should be established and implemented to ensure that materials are assembled properly and that they are assigned to the appropriate destination. Procedures should include use of:

- bar codes;

- checklists;

- verification/QA procedures (e.g., lot sampling); and

- tracking processes.

10.1.5 A process to reconcile original orders and any additional orders should be established and documented.

**10.2 A process should be established and implemented to ensure the accurate labeling of all completed packages.**

This procedure should include information regarding how box sequencing (e.g., Box 1 of N) and the total number of boxes will be displayed. Labels should:

- contain address and contact information that matches the most up-to-date information provided; and

- be placed on boxes according to specifications agreed upon by the client and the service provider.

**10.3 Expedited packaging and shipping requirements should be developed and agreed upon by the client and the service provider, and should be identified in instructions/documentation and disseminated accordingly.**

**10.4 A plan should be developed and implemented for packaging and shipping of breach forms, if necessary.**

**10.5 A process should be established and implemented to ensure documentation is created and maintained for all completed orders.**

10.5.1 Access to documentation, including security checklists and packing lists, should be established for the service provider's management personnel to respond to client inquiries.

10.5.2 A packing list for each box, as well as a report or schematic describing the layout of materials included, should be available to the individual receiving the shipment.

10.5.3   An inventory of materials shipped should be regularly updated and available in an agreed-upon schedule.

10.5.4   An inventory of materials in the vendor warehouse should be regularly updated and available in an agreed-upon schedule (see Chapter 11).

# CHAPTER 11. DISTRIBUTION OF MATERIALS AND CHAIN OF CUSTODY MANAGEMENT

## Introduction

At different times in the assessment life cycle, materials and electronic files need to be transported, distributed, and managed between different service providers, client facilities, schools, and students. The most prevalent example is the production of test materials (e.g., test books, answer documents, coordinator manuals, CDs and other forms of digital products, and other ancillaries) by different service providers and subcontractors. These materials must be brought together to be assembled into packages and shipped. Due to the sensitive nature of the materials, a chain of custody must be maintained at every step, from the production of the materials to delivery at the testing location, to ensure the security and integrity of the assessment content. The management of this chain of custody should be apparent in and between all steps of the materials handling process (e.g., production, printing, packaging, distribution, and return or retrieval of test materials). It also should be apparent in the printing and distribution of reports (see Chapter 17). It is imperative that all hand-offs, both physical and electronic, are managed appropriately between affected stakeholders, including the service provider, subcontractors, departments of education, districts, school officials, and students. This chapter describes best practices for the distribution and hand-off of materials between key stakeholders and reinforces the management of the materials through the chain of custody. Generally, it covers practices to be referenced when materials are distributed from one stakeholder to another. Additional practices related to the administration of technology-based assessments are covered in Chapter 15.

11.1 All changes in the custody of materials will be identified in advance of program implementation. A change in custody occurs when different stakeholders are responsible for separate tasks/activities that occur along the assessment lifecycle. Each task is owned by a stakeholder and, as such, each stakeholder is responsible to be a sender and/or receiver of materials. **A plan detailing processes and procedures should be developed and documented from distribution, to onsite materials management, and return. All participants involved in handling test materials should be trained on appropriate roles and responsibilities.**

11.1.1 Stakeholders responsible for sending or receiving materials include the service provider, client, subcontractors, state, district, or school officials, and students.

11.1.2 Changes in custody may also occur between different processes, such as content production, materials printing (including proofs), packaging and assembly, distribution to districts and schools, distribution within schools and classrooms, delivery to the scoring service provider (return instructions provided), delivery to the secure test materials service provider (return instructions provided), and production and assembly of paper reports.

11.2 **All stakeholders will ensure the security, integrity, and accuracy of materials shipped, transported, received, and stored, while maintaining their portion of the chain of custody.**

11.2.1 These definitions describe the links in the chain of custody:

- Shipper: any stakeholder sending materials to another stakeholder;

- Sender: any stakeholder transmitting files to another stakeholder;

- Transporter: any transportation provider (not applicable for electronic files); and

- Receiver: any stakeholder receiving materials from another stakeholder.

11.2.2 All stakeholder facilities must be secure. This includes the use of security personnel, restricted areas based on employee type, and security of computer systems receiving test materials. Security is discussed in more detail in Chapter 8.

11.2.3 Materials and electronic files must be protected from damage that may affect their use, such as exposure to the weather, direct sunlight, and other variances in atmosphere, electronic surges, and viruses/malware.

11.2.4 Shipper responsibilities should include:

- using appropriate packaging materials to protect both paper and electronic media (e.g., CDs, USB drives);

- ensuring accurate quantities are shipped;

- using packing lists reflecting accurate material titles and correct quantities;

- using a bill of lading for freight shipments;

- ensuring accurate information on shipping labels;

- ensuring shipping labels are visible and identifiable on each package;

- using appropriate method of traceable transportation (e.g., ground, express) to ensure delivery on or by expected receipt date;

- using pallet maps, if appropriate;

- using material handling checklists for secure and nonsecure materials;

- obtaining all required signatures on shipped packages; and

- providing electronic tracking of shipments.

11.2.5 Sender responsibilities should include:

- initiating or arranging for a receiver to initiate a transmission;

- using appropriate file encryption techniques;

- using secure method of file transfer (e.g., secure line, SFTP); and

- notification of transmission of files and acknowledging the recipient's acknowledgement of the transmission.

11.2.6 Transporter responsibilities should include:

- ensuring packages accepted match the bill of lading;
- reviewing credentials or permissions allowing transportation;
- using appropriate vehicles for security and to protect packages;
- accommodating dock restrictions of the shipper and receiver;
- providing traceability of packages; and
- obtaining all required signatures.

11.2.7 Receiver responsibilities should include:

- following procedures and protocols established for the program for acknowledging receipt of the materials, (e.g., date, time, signature);
- checking the physical condition of materials;
- following procedures and protocols established by the service provider if materials are damaged;
- ensuring accepted packages match bill of lading;
- ensuring box contents match the packing list;
- storing received materials in a secured location with limited access (see Chapter 8);
- initiating an inquiry to acquire a materials file from a sender;
- using appropriate file decryption techniques;
- using secure method of file transfer (e.g., secure line, SFTP); and
- notification of transmission of files and acknowledging the sender's transmission.

**11.3** **State, district, and school officials will establish a chain of custody to ensure that materials and electronic files are received, accounted for, and distributed for test administration, and returned, if appropriate, to the service provider following test administration.**

11.3.1 Test coordinators should account for materials received from the service provider, including conducting the following steps:

- comparing and verifying that the materials are organized by teacher or grade group using the packing list;

- making use of the secure material checklist to verify materials; and

- reporting any missing, damaged, or defective materials according to established procedures.

11.3.2 Test coordinators should account for electronic files received from the service provider, including conducting the following steps:

- verifying that all necessary files have been received; and

- reporting any missing or defective files, according to established procedures.

11.3.3 Protocols should be developed to deal with the distribution of materials among test coordinators and test administrators to ensure all materials get to the correct students.

11.3.4 When additional materials or files are needed, processes should be established for requesting those materials, including specifying to whom the request is to be made.

11.3.5 Following test administration, scorable and secure materials should be reassembled for return, according to the instructions provided by the service provider.

11.3.6 Administered tests and related secure materials should be returned/shipped back to the service provider, according to the instructions and schedule provided by the service provider.

11.3.7  Once student responses are transmitted to the service provider, the secure files will be removed from all local systems (e.g., work stations, servers).

11.3.8  The client and the service provider should jointly establish procedures for recovering materials, including administered tests, from tardy districts and schools.

11.3.9  The client and the service provider should jointly establish procedures for recovering assessment data not transmitted/received as expected

# CHAPTER 12. RECEIVING, CHECK-IN, AND PROCESSING OF MATERIALS

## Introduction

When materials (e.g., test booklets, answer documents, CDs, DVDs) are received at a scoring site, they must be prepared for processing. Scorable materials should be sorted out and/or verified and then compiled to ensure that they are grouped correctly prior to scanning or other scoring options. This preparation often includes accounting for each district and ensuring that the scorable materials are aligned correctly under the appropriate header sheets. It is important to maintain scorable materials within the correct organizational hierarchy (e.g. state, district, school, classroom) to ensure accurate data management and aggregate/disaggregate reporting.

Secure materials should be sorted and grouped, which usually occurs at several levels, such as by class or grade within a school, and by school within a district. This allows for correct accounting and reconciliation for each group after security reports are produced.

12.1   A process will be established and implemented to ensure accurate receipt, check-in, and processing of materials at the processing center. The following considerations should be reviewed and documented.

   12.1.1   Receipt from all districts and schools should be verified and recorded to include the total number of packages shipped.

   12.1.2   Scorable and secure nonscorable materials arriving at the same location should be entered into separate workflows.

   12.1.3   Scorable materials should be checked into the workflow to be tracked through processing.

   12.1.4   Processing rules and specifications should be implemented.

   12.1.5   Processes should be established with clients to communicate and resolve issues.

12.1.6 Training protocols for materials handlers should be implemented.

12.1.7 Documents should be removed from packages by trained staff and prepared for scanning according to agreed upon requirements.

12.1.8 Documents should be sorted by district, building, and teacher/grade group.

12.1.9 Documents should be aligned based on orientation and location of identifying marks.

12.1.10 Extraneous materials should be removed.

12.1.11 Document counts should be verified.

12.1.12 Processing rules to ensure that buildings are shown within the correct district should be established.

12.1.13 Processing rules to ensure that teacher/grade groups exist within the correct building should be established.

12.1.14 Documents should be stacked or bundled to ensure hierarchy integrity and to provide the ability to rebuild the stacks if documents come out of order.

**12.2 A process will be established to reconcile and report any missing packages or material (see Chapter 11).**

# CHAPTER 13. SCANNING AND POST-SCANNING EDITING

## Introduction

Best practices in this chapter describe the processes and procedures that are necessary to ensure accuracy and efficiency throughout the service provider's scanning and editing of student answer documents that contain both selected-response and constructed-response areas. Generally, it is the responsibility of the service provider and the client to do the following:

- provide an environment that achieves the highest possible degree of accuracy and efficiency throughout this critical phase; and
- develop detailed specifications for administration protocols and the editing rules to be applied to student demographic and item response information.

Additionally, best practices are recommended for clients performing their own scanning of answer documents.

**13.1   A process should be established jointly between the client and the service provider for accurate and efficient scanning.**

   13.1.1   Documents to be scanned should meet production specifications, as defined by current and relevant technologies. For example, specifications should include rules and procedures for the use of:

- anchor points;

- timing tracks; and

- dropout ink.

   13.1.2   Protocols established for the test administration and security of test materials, as described in Chapters 4, 8, and 9, should be reviewed for application in the scanning process, including:

- appropriate student writing/marking instrument directions; and

- appropriate response areas on the student answer document.

13.1.3    Documents should be scanned in a secure, climate-controlled environment. Documents should be evaluated for moisture content and have a process in place for acclimating documents prior to scanning so that moisture content does not impact scanning results.

13.1.4    The scanning hardware and supporting software should be calibrated on an agreed-upon schedule and the calibration procedures should be documented.

13.1.5    Scanner operators should be trained and training should be documented.

13.1.6    A specifications document that delineates the attributes of the scanning process (e.g., how a mark is recognized), such as nonconforming marks (e.g., multiple, incomplete or light marks) or erasures, should be created and agreed upon by the client and the service provider.

13.1.7    A procedure which outlines how to reconcile nonconforming marks or incomplete student information should be established.

13.1.8    Processes should be established and used to verify the accuracy of the scanning hardware and supporting software. These processes should include use of:

- An appropriate calibration process (e.g., test deck with known values or other process) to verify the accuracy of data collected on each scanner;

- a User Acceptance Test (UAT); and

- an established hardware maintenance protocol.

13.1.9    When a scanner fails to meet calibration requirements, a plan should be in place to intervene and to identify documents and data potentially affected. A plan to rescan affected documents, if required, should be developed and implemented.

**13.2**   **A process should be established to ensure that student response document (e.g., scannable booklet or form) integrity is maintained during the scanning process (e.g., the correct pages are scanned, in order, and the page counts match the booklet specifications).**

13.2.1   The documents should be checked for total page count.

13.2.2   The documents should be checked for image completeness and clarity.

13.2.3   A litho code, bar code, or other identifying strategy should be used on each page or sheet.

**13.3**   **A process should be established to ensure that all documents requiring scanning are scanned or otherwise reconciled.**

13.3.1   Protocols should be developed and implemented for handling contaminated materials (e.g., bodily fluids).

13.3.2   An exception-handling process for damaged or other unscannable documents (e.g., torn documents, substance spilled on a document, extraneous ink or highlighter marks, stray marks) should be developed and documented. This process should include:

- key entry with verification;

- flatbed image scanning; and

- alternative processing, if applicable.

13.3.3   A procedure should be in place to reconcile the number of scannable documents received with the number of documents actually scanned.

**13.4**   **An editing process should be established to ensure accurate collection of data from scanned documents.**

13.4.1   A specification document should be created that delineates how a mark read by the scanner is identified and edited. This document should cover the following issues:

- identification of appropriate values for all edited fields (e.g., names as A-Z, multiple choice options as 1-4);

- multiple marks;

- omitted marks (i.e., leading, trailing, or embedded);

- blanks; and

- editing quality control rules.

13.4.2 A user acceptance test (UAT) of the editing software should be completed prior to implementation of the full production system.

13.4.3 Editors should be trained and training should be documented.

**13.5 A contingency plan or system, approved by both the service provider and the client, should be developed and implemented so that any issues encountered in scanning will not delay scoring and reporting.**

13.5.1 Processes and systems should be in place for transferring scanned data for scoring.

13.5.2 An exception process for data anomalies (e.g., multiple marks, missing data) should be developed and documented to:

- verify that scanned data files meet previously established requirements before submitting them for scoring;

- confirm back to the originating (sending) system that the data files are ready for the scoring system; and

- archive copies of the data files for contingency purposes.

13.5.3 Reconciliation of the number of records sent and those received should occur before reporting.

**13.6 When scanning occurs at the client level (e.g., school, district, state, or other entity) an internal production scanning process should be in place for capturing selected responses from student answer documents. This process should include the elements recommended for service provider scanning in the previous sections of this chapter as well as:**

13.6.1     A contingency plan or system should be developed and implemented so that any issues encountered in scanning will not delay scoring and reporting.

13.6.2     Use of header sheets to indicate document and student N-counts that can be associated with the appropriate district, school, and teacher/classroom for N-count reconciliation, if needed.

13.6.3     A process and system for transferring scanned data for scoring.

13.6.4     An exception process for data anomalies (e.g., multiple marks, missing data) should be developed, documented, and adhered to by the client.

13.6.5     A verification process to compare the header sheets to the number of student records and/or answer documents processed.

13.6.6     Reconciliation of the number of documents received to the number of processed records should occur before reporting.

# CHAPTER 14. SCORING

## Introduction

This chapter includes best practices related to scoring both paper-based and technology-based assessments. The scoring process includes constructed and selected-response scoring, as well as the application of scoring rules, production of raw scores, matching of scores for students, provision of data for equating and scaling, and calculating of the final scores for reporting (see Chapter 17). The exchange of scoring rubrics and student scores also requires that the client and the service provider evaluate and implement a process to maximize the interoperability of systems for exchanging and sharing such data.

The scoring methods employed are dependent upon the item types that are selected for the assessment. Using objective items allows for a machine to score the items because the responses fall into a defined set of correct answers. Constructed-response items elicit student responses that can be scored by humans, machines, or an artificial intelligence (AI) engine. Items with constructed responses that cannot be machine scored should be scored by trained and qualified human scorers, by a trained AI scoring engine, or both.

The quality of constructed-response scoring remains an important component of the overall scoring process, from preparation through the operational scoring. Scores assigned to students who respond to constructed-response items must be reliable and ensure an accurate reflection of student performance on these items, whether scored by machine, human scorers or an AI scoring system. Depending on how constructed responses are scored, there are several factors that impact scores, including scorer training and calibration, artificial intelligence engine training and calibration, scorer staffing processes (e.g., background, content experience), and quality assurance processes. Also, appropriate consideration should be given to associated elements of constructed-response scoring, such as security and confidentiality of student information.

**14.1** **The client and the service provider will determine the methods of scoring based on different item types.**

    14.1.1    Objective items (e.g., multiple choice, gridded response) are machine scored from a set of limited answers using an answer key.

    14.1.2    Constructed-response items may be machine scored (e.g. fill-in the blank) or they may be complex items (e.g., essay, short-answer) that need either human scorers or AI engines for scoring.

    14.1.3    Technology-enhanced items use practices made possible by technology to enhance item presentation and response capture capabilities. These items may include simulations, e-portfolios, and interactive games, that must have a set of rubrics defined for either human or AI scoring. Scoring methods require setting up the set of correct and/or acceptable responses during the item development phase, including any relevant decision trees.

    14.1.4    Performance tasks ask students to demonstrate their skills through open-ended and real-world tasks – delivered on paper or digitally. These items are typically complex, and require the development of a set of rubrics defined for scoring. They can be scored according to the same procedures for scoring any constructed-response, using machine scoring, AI, or human scoring, whichever is appropriate for the task.

**14.2** **Processes should be established to ensure the accuracy and reliability of objective response scoring.**

    14.2.1    Scoring processes for objective items are dependent upon the delivery method. Individual item answer keys or limited answer sets are created during item development.

            •    Linear fixed form testing – the test form answer keys are created prior to administration and applied when each test form is scored.

- Linear-on-the-fly testing (LOFT) – the test form answer keys are created at the time each test form is generated and applied at the time of scoring.

- Computer adaptive testing (CAT) – the individual item answer keys are applied as each item is administered.

14.2.2 Student responses are collected and scored using the following steps.

- Raw item responses are compared to the item answer key or limited answer set and a raw item score (i.e., correct, incorrect, partially correct, or omitted) is produced.

- Raw test scores are produced and may be distinguished by section, by subject, or simply by total score.

- For linear fixed form or LOFT testing, once a sufficient volume of scores is available, item analysis can be conducted for quality control purposes. The data resulting from the scoring may also be used for scaling and equating. The client and the service provider should define client involvement in the item analysis and review process.

**14.3 Processes should be established to perform human scoring of constructed responses, where applicable, and for such uses as the client and the service provider agree.**

14.3.1 These processes should include proper preparation for scoring constructed responses by human scorers.

- A plan for scorer training and qualifying, including appropriate certification (e.g., for an assessment mode, testing session, and/or item type), should be documented and approved by the client.

- General scorer hiring standards should be documented and available to the client and, where appropriate, other stakeholders.

- Scorer training and the process of scorer qualifying to score should be based on input from subject-matter experts in the area being scored, and approved by the client. Ongoing feedback from scoring leaders helps scorers score responses according to testing program standards.

- Scorer qualification statistics should be collected, documented, and used for ongoing evaluation and feedback to scorers from their scoring leader. Scorer data may be used to maintain their qualifications and to ensure the client's scoring standards are met.

- Materials used for scorer training and qualifying should represent student responses across the entire population of possible student response submissions. Materials should include rubrics, exemplars covering the full range of score points, types and styles of writing, information on disregarding cues related to disability, English learner status, or accommodations that are unrelated to scoring criteria, and other relevant considerations, such as topic-specific notes that comprise scoring considerations raised by the particular features of each topic.

- Field-test scoring of constructed-response responses should mimic operational scoring, to the extent possible, and ensure the use of similar scorer selection protocols; and similar training and qualification standards.

14.3.2 These processes should ensure reliable operational scoring results of constructed responses by human scorers. These results should meet predefined target expectations and specifications agreed upon by the client and the service provider.

- Student handwritten responses to constructed-response items should be scored by trained and qualified human scorers.

- The plan for scorer training and qualifying should be documented and approved by the client.

- Quality checks should be conducted throughout the scoring process (e.g. use of double reading, back reading/read behinds, trend monitoring).

- Individual and group scorer performance results should be measured and analyzed regularly.

- When performance of an individual scorer and/or a group of scorers falls outside of target expectations, corrective action should be taken. This may include retraining of scorers and rescoring of selected student responses. The process for making a decision to retrain scorers, and/or rescore selected student responses, should be established ahead of time and should be driven by score quality considerations, and should be agreed upon by the client and the service provider.

- Validity papers or check-sets, consisting of previously scored student responses, may be administered to check on scorer accuracy.

- Scores assigned by scorers to selected student responses should be confirmed with scores from other expert scorers or by artificial intelligence scoring methods, as a mechanism to monitor scorer accuracy according to client specifications.

- Inter-rater reliability data should be collected by sampling a percentage of papers for additional ratings. These additional ratings may be performed by other qualified scorers, expert scorers, or by computer using artificial intelligence procedures. If the contract requires resolution when there are differences between scores, a procedure for resolving score discrepancies (sometimes called adjudication) should be developed, agreed upon by the client and the service provider, documented, and followed during scoring.

- Any measure or analysis used to check accuracy and reliability of the scoring process should be made available for the client's review.

- A plan for the machine scoring of any multiple-choice items included with the constructed-response items should be developed and approved by the service provider and the client. As part of this plan, the programming of the answer key should be checked by staff, independent of programmers.

**14.4 Processes should be established to perform automated scoring of constructed responses using AI engines, where applicable, and for such uses as the client and the service provider agree.**

14.4.1 These processes should include the proper preparation for scoring constructed responses by AI engines.

- Processes should be established with input from test designers, technologists, and scoring experts to ensure that all benefits and/or tradeoffs specific to the item and task (e.g., cost, complexity, retraining and recalibration frequency, delivery times) are considered.

- AI training should utilize student responses representative of the entire population of possible student response submissions. The training and calibration of the AI engine should include a full range of score points (especially at the cut points), types and styles of writing, and other relevant considerations.

14.4.2   These processes should ensure reliable results of operational scoring of constructed responses by AI engines. These results should meet predefined target expectations and specifications agreed upon by the client and the service provider.

- When AI engines are used in place of human scoring, or for confirmation or quality control of human scoring, scoring procedures should meet the same standards for accuracy and reliability that exist for human scoring of the same item type. Methods for the calibration of the artificial intelligence scoring engines, and evidence that the engine meets accuracy and reliability standards, should be documented.

- AI validation should represent student responses representative of the entire population of possible student response submissions. Validation should include a range of score points, types and styles of writing, and other relevant considerations.

- AI performance results should be measured and analyzed regularly. A process should be established to permit recalibration and/or retraining, as appropriate.

- Any measure or analysis used to check accuracy and reliability of the scoring process should be made available for the client's review.

**14.5   Processes will be established to accurately match and combine scoring results for all responses for each student. These results should meet predefined target expectations and specifications agreed upon by the client and the service provider.**

14.5.1   A process will be in place to match the raw objective response scores and the constructed response scores with registration data. Unmatched data (i.e. response data that cannot be linked to a student) will be resolved through a defined process, likely to be manual.

14.5.2    A process will be in place to apply the scoring rules that define how the objective and constructed response scores should be combined to create the composite score for the particular test. Scoring rules include the production test answer key, aggregation, and score assignments rules.

**14.6    The client and the service provider should evaluate how well the available data exchange standards support the necessary information for scoring. Based on that evaluation, they should establish and document interoperable procedures to exchange/share scoring information. Data required to calculate final test scores should include item level scoring information (e.g., answer keys, rubrics), item mappings, and weightings to determine total scores and "strand" scores. In addition, score tables may be provided to transform a raw score into a scale score or a normative score. Score tables may also be provided for determining performance levels and pass/fail indicators.**

**14.7    Quality control processes should be established and approved by the service provider and the client to perform verifications of the scoring of items that are included on the test (e.g., read-behinds, answer key checks, test decks).**

14.7.1    The specifications document used in the scanning process should be referenced during verification (see 13.4).

14.7.2    Original training procedures and materials should be used to qualify individuals to perform verifications.

14.7.3    Original answer documents should be used for verification.

14.7.4    All discrepancies (including defects) should be tracked, investigated, and documented.

14.7.5    Performance metrics should be collected to determine the rate of discrepancy.

14.7.6    A plan for corrective action should be developed, if needed.

14.7.7    The agreed-upon corrective action plan (e.g., use of root cause analysis, discrepancy tracking tools) should be used when discrepancies are discovered.

14.7.8    Student data resulting from scoring shall be considered secure information (see Chapter 8).

14.7.9    The service provider should provide for scoring of the breach form, if it is within contract scope.

14.7.10   Storage and retention of original answer documents and verification documentation should follow the plan established and agreed upon by the service provider and the client.

**14.8    Procedures should be established to identify, evaluate, and, if necessary, escalate alert papers (e.g., disturbing content, potential cheating, security concerns) to the client.**

14.8.1    The client and the program service provider should establish and agree upon rules that guide the scoring service provider in identifying alert papers and maintaining confidentiality.

14.8.2    Communication to the client or the client's representative should promptly follow discovery of any alert papers and should include confirmation of the questionable content by scoring leaders, scoring directors, or other service provider scoring officials.

14.8.3    Rules about reporting alert papers to appropriate governing authorities of the client should be developed and followed by the service provider and the client.

**14.9    The procedures established for the scoring process should ensure that confidentiality is maintained and student identifiable information is securely controlled.**

14.9.1    Scorers should only see the student response and not any student identifiable information.

14.9.2    Standard security procedures should be followed during scoring and other processing (see chapter 8).

**14.10   A plan should be developed and agreed upon by the service provider and the client that delineates the process for late batch scoring (batches of student responses that are provided to the scoring vendor after the established, agreed-upon window). The plan should include:**

- date ranges in which late batch scoring will be accepted for processing without additional fee;

- date ranges in which late batch scoring will be accepted for processing with additional fee;

- date ranges in which late batch scoring will not be accepted for processing;

- a communication plan for the acceptance or rejection of late batch scoring requests;

- a method for logging results from late batches;

- a method for communicating late batch scoring results;

- the use of original training procedures and materials to qualify individuals to perform late batch scoring; and

- a method for incorporating late batch results into appropriate data sets and score reports.

**14.11 A plan and process should be developed and agreed upon by the service provider and the client for rescoring, score verification requests, and appeals. The plan should include a schedule and methods for:**

- rescoring based on score verification requests or appeals;

- logging results from rescoring;

- communicating rescoring results;

- training procedures and materials to qualify individuals to perform rescores; and

- updating data sets and score reports and informing other users of updated results.

# CHAPTER 15. TECHNOLOGY-BASED ASSESSMENTS AND TECHNICAL SUPPORT

## Introduction

This chapter describes operational best practices for technology-based assessments, or those assessments delivered using a computer or other "Net-centric" device possessing computer capability (e.g., hand-held devices, tablets, cellular telephones). While the evolution of technology-based assessments has continued since their inception in the late 1970s, proliferation into large-scale assessment is more recent. Service providers have expanded their product lines to include technology-based assessments, and clients and school districts are in various stages of preparation and/or implementation. As such, some procedures and processes outlined in this chapter to assist the client and school districts in preparing for and delivering technology-based assessments are not as time-tested as other operational best practices. Best practices addressing the administration of technology-based assessments are found in Chapter 9.

The challenges associated with implementing large-scale technology-based assessments are shared by the service provider, the client, and school districts. As school districts attempt to develop adequate and consistent infrastructure across their testing locations to support technology-based assessments, the client and the service provider must continue to develop interoperable solutions that can utilize low-cost devices and emerging technologies, while maintaining a secure and standardized testing experience for students.

15.1    Requirements for technology infrastructure needed by the client, school districts, and the service provider to support technology-based assessments must be clearly documented and explained. The following specifications and requirements should be considered:

- descriptions of:
    - compatible and/or recommended network platforms;
    - minimum and recommended network configurations;

- minimum and recommended bandwidth demands for the service provider's solution; and

- desired type(s) of technology-based assessments, items, and permissible accommodations;

• a plan to address the interoperability of service provider, client, and district systems, including hardware, software and various data elements and data transfers;

• details or recommendations for using the service provider's assessment software and/or systems with various infrastructure devices and networking technologies, such as:

- Domain Name System (DNS) servers, enterprise firewalls, content filters, and port blocking packages;

- network load balancers, caching devices, and bandwidth management devices; and

- network and layered security applications, network management and/or monitoring applications, and enterprise antivirus software;

• a process (e.g., a regularly conducted survey) for collecting data about current technology, including capabilities of the client and its school districts, when evaluating readiness for technology-based assessments; and

• a method or application for load testing or stress testing of the service provider's hosting infrastructure (if applicable) and the infrastructure of the client, school districts, and school buildings. The load or stress test methods should be scalable to ensure current and projected infrastructure demands can be assessed. Such infrastructure demands may vary over time due to increased test volume and/or new test types (e.g., computer adaptive testing, simulations, animations, multimedia, embedded accessibility options).

**15.2 Requirements for devices and software to be used by the client, school districts, and the service provider to deliver and manage secure, technology-based assessments, should**

---

**be clearly documented and explained. These requirements will be made available in manuals or other published documents that are shared with stakeholders via an established communication protocol, and should include the following:**

- descriptions of platforms and environments (e.g., PC-compatible, Mac-compatible, Linux, Android, iOS, thin-client) required to support the delivery of secure, technology-based assessments with minimum requirements, as agreed upon by the service provider and the client, including:

    - minimum and recommended processor requirements (type and speed);

    - minimum and recommended memory requirements;

    - supported operating systems (types and versions);

    - supported web browsers (types and versions);

    - minimum and recommended audio and visual requirements (e.g., graphics and sound cards);

    - additional software requirements, including names, required version numbers, and license requirements (if relevant) for any necessary applications, browser plug-ins, players, etc.; and

    - minimum screen resolution and size requirements for displays;

- descriptions of any necessary or recommended supporting devices, such as printers, scanners, alternative display devices, and alternative input devices (e.g., stylus, adaptive keyboard, camera);

- detailed instructions for downloading, installing, configuring, and uninstalling any required software with troubleshooting tips and details for obtaining installation support. Options for deploying or configuring necessary software should be documented and presented with pros and cons of installation and configuration decisions (e.g., client installation versus server installation, options for temporary directories, wired versus wireless, lab configurations);

- details and/or recommendations for using the service provider's assessment software and/or systems with various devices and installed applications or plug-ins, such as the following:

  - pop-up blockers, anti-spam applications, anti-virus software, and personal or device-level firewalls;

  - personal or device-level content filters, layered security applications, and image restoration applications used to return a device to an original state;

  - remote monitoring and management software (e.g., N-central, On-Sight, NetSupport School) and other applications running in the background on devices; and

  - specific end user instructions in the event of a service interruption due to software, Internet, or LAN malfunction; and

- details of a procedure or an application, such as a "wizard", to verify device requirements, proper installation and configuration of software, and other necessary components, prior to testing.

15.3 **The client and the service provider should work together to determine the assistive technologies that will be available for technology-based assessments. Requirements and recommendations for integrating assistive technologies to maximize accessibility to technology-based assessments should be made available to school districts (see Chapter 19). These requirements may include the following:**

- details and/or recommendations for types of available assistive technologies that are compatible and interoperable with the service provider's test delivery solution and any relevant stakeholder's systems;

- minimum and recommended technical requirements and recommendations for installing and implementing compatible assistive technologies;

- consultation with assistive technology professionals and psychometric professionals should be considered regarding the use of assistive technologies for the administration of technology-based assessments; and

- a review of accommodations available for students to access nontechnology-based assessments is recommended to consider whether similar and appropriate accommodations are available for students to access technology-based assessments.

**15.4** **All technologies and procedures used by the client, school districts, and the service provider must support test security and the maintenance of a secure test environment throughout the technology-based test administration (see Chapter 8). These procedures should include the following:**

- maintaining appropriate encryption of test content, responses, and associated data throughout all data transmissions and during all periods of storage;

- maintaining the chain of custody for all secure test materials and data throughout the test administration process;

- implementing appropriate network security practices and technology (e.g., firewalls, protocols) to prevent unauthorized access to secure test materials during the test administration;

- implementing appropriate technology and/or administration procedures to prevent inappropriate access to external content or sharing of secure test content by students during their test administration; and

- implementing appropriate technology and/or administration procedures to control and track access to secure test content and data by test administrators and test examiners.

**15.5** **Technical support for technology-based assessments should be made available by the service provider to the client through toll-free telephone support, email support, and/or support documentation available via a web site. Additional considerations of technical support may include:**

- technical support services should be provided by persons with knowledge of support and customer services, who are specifically trained in the technology-based assessments, systems, procedures, and tools they will be supporting for the client (including, where appropriate under the contract, for school districts). Different levels or tiers of technical support may be implemented by the service provider to increase efficiency of responses, and options should be available to the client in the event advanced, on-site technical assistance is needed;

- roles and responsibilities between the service provider and the client should be defined regarding types of questions to be answered by the service provider versus inquiries referred to the client due to policy considerations (e.g., granting secure system access, changing permissions and/or passwords, specific assessment policies);

- guidelines should be established between the service provider and the client regarding availability of technical support (hours and days);

- the service provider and the client should consider how real-time technical support will be provided and sustained for on-site test examiners, test proctors, and technology specialists to address issues occurring during operational student testing;

- a searchable database containing potential responses should be available to service provider technical support staff, which should be updated regularly as assessment systems, technologies, policies, and procedures are revised;

- requests for support and subsequent responses should be documented and logged into a database, which may include unique assigned issue numbers with date and time initiated, support requested, identity and contact information of requestor, documented responses and communications with requestor, and status. This database should be updated regularly for effectiveness of responses and to identify trends, emerging issues, and potential training needs;

- a communication plan should exist within the service provider's organization so planned and unplanned system changes are communicated promptly to technical support staff, and repeated issues experienced by technical support staff are communicated to appropriate service provider staff and/or client staff;

- technical support expectations should be agreed upon and response metrics monitored by the service provider and shared with the client. Metrics may include numbers of requests, call and/or email response times, number of abandoned calls, types of requests, time to issue closure, etc. Contingency plans for managing high call volume during peak testing times should exist; and

- a method for collecting client and school district feedback regarding accuracy and timeliness of technical support should be established with collected data reviewed on a regular basis.

**15.6** **The technical support documents should include information about suggested computer lab configurations. Many school computer labs are set up to support instruction and not assessment. These labs may need to be reconfigured. Proctors of technology-based assessments should be informed about how to reconfigure the labs, how long the reconfiguration will take, and any additional precautions (such as vision blockers) that should be taken prior to testing.**

**15.7** **Training about technology-based assessments should be made available by the service provider(s) to the client for expected delivery to school districts within the contract scope. Training should be available in multiple modes, such as web-based training, face-to-face training, recorded multimedia modules, training documents, etc. Additional training should include, but not be limited to:**

- addressing specific topics related to assessment and technology, as well as specific audiences, such as test administrators, test proctors, technology staff, teachers, students, and parents/community members;

- providing a training environment that mimics conditions anticipated during live testing for technology-based assessments, for use by the client and school districts, and that should allow training and practice by test administrators, computer lab coordinators, and proctors, but must not expose secure test content or confidential student data;

- providing a training/practice environment for use by students and other stakeholders, that should include keyboarding and navigating the technology-based assessments, using associated technology-based tools, and experiencing various item types and formats that will be used during live testing prior to a test administration, but must not expose secure test content or confidential student data;

- developing and implementing training materials for technology-based assessments, including the following topics:

  - a description and details of suggested roles and responsibilities (e.g., for test administrators, computer lab coordinators, test proctors, technology specialists);

  - resource documents or checklists to ensure all necessary tasks are completed by appropriate staff before, during, and after testing;

  - test security practices and policies to be implemented before, during, and after testing (see Chapter 8);

  - technology troubleshooting procedures, and suggested responses to likely scenarios and unexpected events, before, during, and after testing;

  - a process for regularly evaluating and receiving feedback from the client and school districts about the various training opportunities and resources; and

- a description of the location of user guides, FAQs, and other resource documents, as well as a process that will be used for updating them.

**15.8** **Performance of the service provider's software and systems is critical to a successful implementation of technology-based assessments and must be benchmarked and regularly monitored. Systems must be adaptable and scalable to respond to increases in assessment volume, changes in types of assessments, and changes in technology. Procedures for monitoring system performance should be established and implemented, including the following:**

- a formal service level agreement (SLA) communicating baseline performance expectations, as agreed upon by the service provider and the client. Performance expectations should include factors such as hours of system availability, maximum allowable downtime, expected incident response times, expected incident communication paths, performance metrics, etc.;

- performance metrics to be monitored and reported, as agreed upon by the service provider and the client covering before, during, and after test administration. This should include the number of concurrent administrative users, number of concurrent students taking tests, application and database server performance, system latency, test interruptions, bandwidth demands, etc. Trend lines should be established to help identify issues, as well as to project changes in system load and performance;

- an action plan developed by the service provider for evaluating and addressing critical system performance issues and a communication plan between the service provider and the client for how critical system performance issues or unplanned outages will be communicated to the client and school districts, as well as internally among service provider staff, such as technical support staff. Multiple modes of communication (e.g., phone, email, web site, independent web site) should be included in the plans to ensure timely and effective message delivery; and

- a schedule for planned system interruptions and maintenance outages agreed upon between the service provider and the client, to be communicated in advance to all system users.

**15.9** **Changes to the service provider's assessment software and/or systems will occur to implement enhancements and to address items such as unexpected issues, changes in technology, interoperability standards, and/or the needs of the client. A process for planning, managing, documenting, testing, and communicating changes to the client and school districts prior to the rollout should be established and implemented. This process should include:**

- providing details, such as impact on project schedules, user interfaces, system documentation, training needs, and policy for all groups as changes are implemented;

- collecting feedback from the client and school districts regarding proposed changes and an evaluation of the change(s) and implementation procedures;

- monitoring hardware and software changes that could impact technology-based assessments, including planned and unplanned changes and communicating relevant details to stakeholders via an established communication protocol; and

- handling changes due to extraordinary circumstances (e.g., severe weather, large-scale emergencies) collaboratively by the client and the service provider with contract and/or SLA changes, as needed.

# CHAPTER 16. TECHNICAL DEFENSIBILITY

## Introduction

The extent to which assessment results are appropriate for their intended use is largely dependent on the implementation of procedures that are consistent with industry standards for technical defensibility, whether tests are administered in a paper-based or technology-based mode. Although these *Operational Best Practices* are not themselves surrogates for the *Standards for Educational and Psychological Testing*, they are intended to be consistent with, and complementary to, those professional and technical standards, by addressing the operational aspects related to a statewide assessment program. Such procedures or practices help ensure that the inferences derived from the assessment results are reliable and valid.

**16.1   Procedures should be established and implemented to ensure that the assessment is consistent with industry standards for technical defensibility.**

   16.1.1   Established standards addressing technical and professional aspects of assessment development should be followed, especially the *Standards for Educational and Psychological Testing*.

   16.1.2   The assessment should adhere to relevant regulations and guidance documents; especially those provided by the United States Department of Education for general, alternate, and English language proficiency accountability assessments (e.g., peer review materials).

   16.1.3   The client is responsible for articulating the intended use(s) of the assessment and for identifying the authorization for the assessment.

   16.1.4   The client and the service provider should jointly review and agree on key technical deliverables, paying special attention to the need for evaluating deliverables for assessments. Key deliverables may include:

- item and form blueprints and specifications;

- procedures and analyses to detect possible bias;

- procedures for evaluating adherence to accessibility and universal design principles;

- rubrics and answer keys, both paper-based and technology-based, to be used for scoring all items;

- field-test sampling plans;

- parameter estimates for all field tested items;

- alignment studies;

- comparability or bridging studies, as needed, for multiple assessment modes (e.g., technology-based and paper-based) and proposed changes to assessments;

- specification of the measurement model and analyses of model fit;

- parameter estimates and other item statistics for operational items;

- standard setting procedures and results;

- equating plan, procedures, and results;

- score-to-scale conversion rules and tables;

- development of vertical scales;

- stability and reliability of subscale scores that may be reported in addition to the total scores;

- analyses of conditional and total-test reliability, as well as classification accuracy and consistency;

- analyses and research conducted to establish the validity of inferences drawn from the assessment results;

- disaggregation of data by predefined groups;

- score report designs and descriptions of performance levels; and

- data analyses, including erasure analysis, and other statistical procedures to detect response integrity violations and other potential security breaches.

16.1.5   The service provider should produce technical reports that document results of creation and use of deliverables.

16.1.6   The contents of any technical reports should be jointly agreed upon by the client and the service provider, in advance of preparation.

16.1.7   The frequency and timeline for production of all reports should be jointly established by the client and the service provider.

16.1.8   The client is responsible for final approval of technical reports and arranging any appropriate access to such materials.

16.1.9   An independent technical advisory committee (TAC), composed of members whose combined background includes familiarity in measuring all student populations, should review and endorse the procedures used in development, scoring, analysis, and reporting, as well as review the technical reports.

# CHAPTER 17. SCORE REPORTING

## Introduction

Score reports are the most visible, yet most misunderstood, products of any assessment. Score reports often are used for high-stakes decisions; consequently, they must be understandable to appropriate stakeholders. The score report provides the information about what the assessment measures; therefore the development and production of score reports should receive the same level of attention to detail and thoughtfulness as that required for test design. This chapter is aimed at ensuring the technical quality of reports and their linkage to assessment program data, regardless of the types of assessments used.

This chapter also covers best practices regarding the purpose and audience for reports, as well as steps for ensuring that reports are accurate, appropriately used, readily available, and accessible to diverse users, to the extent feasible. For most assessment programs, report interpretation guides are written for specific audiences (e.g., parents, teachers, school/district/state administrative staff). The intent of these guides is to provide explanations of the reports that use "nontechnical language" to explain how the results in the reports might be interpreted.

Finally, this chapter deals with best practices covering the distribution of reports and associated guides, both in paper and digital formats, including practices aimed at achieving interoperability in exchanging electronic files and reports among entities sending/receiving score reports.

17.1   **A process should be developed to design and approve program-specific operational score reports and data files that are required for the assessment program, students, parents, teachers, schools, and districts.**

    17.1.1   The process should include determining definitions, specifications, and methods for achieving or improving interoperability in the exchange of each score report and score data file. Such definitions and specifications should include:

- purpose;

- intended audience;

- level of aggregation and/or disaggregation by student groups and subgroups;

- data elements and their definitions;

- business rules for all data elements and calculations;

- performance level and strand/standard information;

- physical design (style and format for reports, file format and record layouts for data files, data elements and available filters for dynamic score reports);

- production and refresh schedules (on-demand or scheduled production);

- report type (static and/or dynamic); and

- delivery mode (digital, printed copy).

17.1.2   The report development process should define, document, and communicate the specific purpose for each score report. The following factors should be considered:

- a report should provide a snapshot of student performance at one point in time, or over time, and its use should be limited to its intended purpose;

- a statement of purpose and guidance regarding use should be included on each report;

- a caution should be provided about potential misuse of each report;

- reports may provide an indication of performance in multiple subject areas;

- reports should be easily understood by the target audience (i.e., reports should be clear, concise, free of jargon);

- reports should be available in different versions (e.g., braille, large print, and languages other than English);

- reports provide schools and districts with program level information; and

- reports are often used in accountability.

17.1.3   The client and the service provider should develop and implement a plan or recommendations to support and communicate to all stakeholders the intended use of score report data for classroom, school district, or program decisions, where appropriate. The following should be considered:

- if student, item, or strand data from the score reports are used, they should only be used in conjunction with other assessment information to guide classroom decisions and instructional focus, and to monitor improvement and growth; and

- if aggregate student data from the score reports are used, they should be used in conjunction with other assessment information to guide program decisions.

17.1.4   A mock-up of every report and data file populated with simulated data should be created for review and approval by the client and the service provider prior to publication. The service provider review should include a psychometric review to ensure appropriate presentation of score information. When feasible, those mock-ups should be shared with all user groups to ascertain if there are problems with understanding or accessibility of the reports.

17.1.5   Report-specific decision rules that define the inclusion specifications and calculations associated with each data element should be developed and agreed upon by the client and the service provider.

17.1.6   If either on-demand score reports or dynamic score reports are required by the client, the service provider must provide minimum hardware and software requirements for accessing such reports.

17.1.7   The client should make the service provider aware of all relevant state and federal laws or regulations pertaining to confidentiality, security, and the reporting of sensitive data. Pertinent laws should be addressed with specific reporting specifications.

**17.2   Prior to reporting, the service provider and the client should review a representative sample of actual score reports, data files, and related materials, as a quality control check of design and decision rules.**

17.2.1   The client and the service provider should agree on a reporting sample and independently verify that all requirements are met.

17.2.2   The client and the service provider should document the approval of each report, whether by signature, electronic means, or otherwise.

**17.3   Specifications for interpretative guides for relevant reports, including style guidelines and content outlines, should be defined.**

17.3.1   The client should identify reports requiring interpretive guides and should indicate the intended audiences for all different versions (e.g., braille, large print, languages other than English).

17.3.2   The client and the service provider should develop a set of stylistic guidelines for development of each guide, including layout specifications.

17.3.3   All numerical reports and data files presented in an interpretive guide should be populated with simulated and reasonably representative data.

17.3.4   The client and the service provider should consider the format (digital and/or printed), availability of the guide, numbers of copies produced, and a distribution plan (if applicable).

17.3.5   The service provider should develop each required interpretive guide for review and approval by the client.

17.3.6    A plan for communicating the availability of
          interpretative guides should be considered, along with
          a method for receiving questions and feedback.

17.3.7    The service provider should regularly review the
          interpretive guides and implement any necessary and/
          or preferred revisions, as approved by the client.

**17.4    The distribution strategy should be defined and agreed
          upon by the client and the service provider for each
          reporting cycle.**

17.4.1    For paper-based materials, the service provider and
          the client should develop an approved specification
          for the number of copies, order of reports,
          distribution, and packaging.

17.4.2    For digital materials, the service provider and the
          client should develop specifications for secure delivery,
          access, and retrieval, including levels of organizational
          access (e.g., state, district, school, class levels), and the
          duration of access.

17.4.3    The distribution strategy and timeline should be
          communicated and a point of contact made available
          to districts and schools for questions regarding
          availability and access to reports and/or data files.

**17.5    Documentation of all reporting specifications should be
          maintained by the service provider and provided to the client
          for approval prior to each reporting cycle.**

17.5.1    Documentation should be inclusive of the definitions
          and specifications for each score report and score data
          file to be produced by the service provider. Change
          logs should be maintained.

17.5.2    An annual (or more frequent) review of the
          documentation should be conducted by the
          service provider and the client to ensure reporting
          requirements and/or data changes are captured
          accurately and in a timely manner.

**17.6**    **A process should be defined and agreed upon by the client and the service provider to address the duration that score reports and data files will be maintained, remain accessible, and be archived.**

    17.6.1    The client should make the service provider aware of all relevant policies, regulations, or laws pertaining to records retention that may affect the required accessibility and archival periods for score reports and data files.

    17.6.2    The specific score reports and data files to be maintained by the service provider should be identified by the client, along with required minimum durations.

    17.6.3    The specific score reports and data files to be archived by the service provider should be identified by the client, along with required minimum durations.

    17.6.4    Related materials, such as interpretive guides, report specifications, and file record layouts, should be archived with relevant score reports and data files.

**17.7**    **A process should be developed and agreed upon by the client and the service provider to address concerns received from districts, schools, and/or parents regarding score report accuracy.**

    17.7.1    The process should include a method for documenting the concern and communicating details between the client and the service provider, so the issue may be researched and investigated.

    17.7.2    The client and the service provider should collaborate to agree on the final resolution and any actions and/or follow-up communications to close the issue.

**17.8**    **The client and the service provider should develop, document, and implement procedures for achieving or improving the interoperability of systems that exchange scoring data and related information. The client and the service provider should evaluate interoperability standards to define how test scores and related assessment information are exchanged across systems.**

17.8.1   Data elements included in the exchange of assessment results vary for different purposes and systems, yet they must be interoperable. Examples include:

- Assessment system. Full details of student assessment results (e.g., item-level analysis, content strand and substrand performance, performance levels) are required in the service provider's system and, as appropriate, in the client's assessment information systems (e.g., data warehouse). These assessment results are combined with student demographics from student information system(s) (see Chapter 18). This may include summary level longitudinal information for year-to-year comparisons and trend analysis;

- Student information system (SIS). Full details of assessment results (combined with student demographics in the SIS) are required for performance analysis of individual students and groups. In addition, consideration must be given to student mobility and resultant record exchange, particularly in light of differing assessments by locale; and

- Transcript exchange. Summary-level information (e.g., total scores, performance levels, and pass/fail indicators, but likely not item-level details) must be available to support student transcripts or official records.

17.8.2   To support interoperable data exchange, in order to allow systems to process and reconcile these data, the following areas related to individual assessment results and individual score reports should be considered:

- individual student data, including unique student identifiers and basic demographics (e.g., name, date of birth);

- test identification and administration data, including the data elements required to identify the assessment form taken and information about the administration;

- test results that are generated (e.g., totals and subscores, raw, scaled, or normative scores, performance levels, and pass/fail indicators);

- longitudinal assessment data, supporting the need for, and use of, growth and/or longitudinal data models adopted by the client;

- aggregated assessment results, supporting how well students are performing compared to other groups of students at the school-, district-, or state-level; and

- scoring attributes derived by the scoring process, such as retest indicators, attemptedness, testing status (e.g., the student was disruptive or was observed cheating), and other similar information.

# CHAPTER 18. DATA MANAGEMENT

## Introduction

There are many points within the assessment life cycle where secure data are stored, changed, transmitted, computed, analyzed, and reported. Data are of the utmost importance to an assessment program because they provide the means by which critical decisions can be made. Ownership of data, whether it is by the client or the service provider, must be clearly understood in order to properly manage the data. Student identifiable information must be isolated and secured to protect the identity of individuals. Procedures and protocols should be developed, followed, and monitored, to maintain accuracy, security, and integrity of the data, as well as to ensure or improve the interoperability of the systems needing to exchange those data.

This chapter addresses the secure management of all assessment data, including points of transfer between stakeholders, along with changes to, archival of, and disposition of the data. The data management strategy is dependent on interoperability of systems (see Chapter 22).

18.1 **Data to be collected and managed should be defined and documented, including the critical time periods in the assessment cycle that these data are likely to be consumed, updated, and purged. Such data and associated meta-data should include, but are not limited to:**

- item data (e.g., content, answer key, item-level tags, statistics);

- enrollment data (e.g., district and school names, grade spans, addresses, student counts, teacher names);

- score recipient data (e.g., score recipient preferences and institutional data, such as mail to and bill to addresses);

- student demographic data (e.g., student names, IDs, gender, DOB, disability, ethnicity) should be included (e.g. within a barcode file, on an answer document, or via an online interface);

- data about specific accommodations used on each assessment;

- student response data (e.g., multiple choice, constructed responses) from an answer document or via an online interface;

- test administration data (e.g., information about the progress of testing, especially with technology-based assessments, post-administration data on timing of testing, and student behavior for technology-based assessments, item-order presentation for adaptive testing); and

- performance data (e.g., student, aggregated, disaggregated) on paper reports, through electronic medium, or via an online interface.

18.2 **The service provider should maintain, and share with appropriate parties, detailed documentation of data elements, data definitions, and usage rules for all collected or derived data, including addressing security and privacy concerns.**

18.3 **Rules should be defined for how to protect, collect, verify, update, share, archive, and dispose of secure data.**

18.3.1 Data are often shared between stakeholders, most often between the client and the service provider, and between district and school staff, where appropriate. Rules should be established on how secure data, including student identifiable information, can be transferred between stakeholders, taking into account legal and regulatory considerations. Examples for how these data are shared include use of secure and managed file transfer sites and service-provider-supplied online interfaces, as well as operational restrictions (e.g., time limited access, password protection). Transferring data via email is not recommended. In an emergency situation when other methods are not available, the data to be emailed must be encrypted.

18.3.2    Where one or more student information systems (SIS) are used and it is feasible to export student enrollment data, detailed interface specification rules should be constructed based on standardized protocols for exchanging such data. The following should be considered when developing the enrollment file:

- formats to receive and process files, including data associations and data interaction (e.g., data models that connect elements together);

- procedures for validating and correcting the incoming information; and

- rules for the appropriate use, storage, retention, and destruction of the data.

18.3.3    File formats must be defined to ensure that data populate correctly during exports and imports across different databases. This formatting must be provided in a detailed file format specification that includes types of fields, number of fields, field lengths, alpha and/or numeric limitations, and descriptions of data elements. Processes should be established to verify formats by using test runs of mock data. In cases where student identifiable information is involved, these data must be masked in any test run.

18.3.4    A secure file transmission solution must be implemented to protect, log, track, and monitor all user access and data transmissions, including confirmation of successful or failed delivery, with the appropriate error conditions indicated upon failure.

18.3.5    When test and report data are presented electronically, personal and confidential IDs and passwords must be used to ensure the authorized level of data access and data updates. IDs must be assigned to each individual. Service provider systems and data access and update controls should adhere to minimum security regulations and guidelines, as established by the client, including requiring timeout on sessions.

18.3.6  Rules should be established on the timing and frequency for when data are collected and transferred, as well as the parties responsible for the verification, updating, and transfer of data. Special attention should be paid to data elements that may change from initial collection to actual use (e.g., school addresses, grade spans, and key contacts can all change without warning).

18.3.7  The client, the service provider, and any third parties should establish rules on how they use and allow data access within their systems. They also must establish procedures for how to detect and/or prevent data intrusions (e.g., password cracking, data transmission hacking, and Structured Query Language [SQL] injection into online systems).

18.3.8  Rules should be established to govern a full-information life-cycle strategy that manages the length of time, format, and level that data should be kept, available, archived, retained, and destroyed from the archive.

18.3.9  A process should be incorporated to allow the client to update data if and when it is reasonable and/or feasible to do so.

18.3.10  A master data management strategy should be developed to ensure that data are managed in a consistent way. The benefits of a successful implementation include:

- minimized data redundancy;

- improved and consistent data quality; and

- consistent reporting and analytics.

18.3.11  The client and the service provider will establish a process of data governance so that data assets are formally managed and data integrity is maintained.

**18.4  The service provider should provide a system that facilitates data management.**

18.4.1 The service provider's systems should include documented processes for authorized administrators to perform the following functions:

- complete data entry of test enrollments via secure electronic uploads of data and manual, real-time data entry of test enrollments via a user-friendly, data entry interface;

- view, modify, add, and remove test enrollments and associated demographic data;

- maintain control of access to test enrollments through managing user accounts or assigning/ removing specific user permissions;

- prevent test enrollments from being revised, added, or deleted at specified times, as determined by the client and/or school districts; and

- implement data entry rules (e.g., specific data elements required to proceed, required format of data elements, disallowing duplicate test enrollments, requiring and validating unique student identifiers), as agreed upon by the service provider and the client or school districts, to prevent or reduce inaccurate data entry.

18.4.2 The service provider and the client should establish and implement procedures for updating the systems based on changing requirements, such as revised student demographic data, revised or new types of test enrollments, revised or new types of student conditions for specific test enrollments, etc.

**18.5 The client and the service provider should develop, document, and implement interoperability procedures for exchanging student information systems (e.g., enrollment) data.**

18.5.1 The client and the service provider should evaluate the interoperability of student test enrollment processes (or student information systems) used to identify the actual students who are scheduled to participate in an assessment administration and/or to identify which specific tests each student is to take, used to determine material personalization and distribution needs, and to identify uniquely students for testing through identifiers, such as student identifications and login credentials. Generally, the enrollment processes collect student demographic data, teacher or class group data, accessibility needs, and any other information necessary to complete scoring or to provide correct accountability and progress data.

18.5.2   Once collected, the student demographics generally provide for a "snapshot" of the data for the test administration. Although this information may continue to change at the source (local information system), it can be used for accountability and data aggregation purposes for that test administration.

**18.6   Individual Student Data. The client and the service provider should evaluate how well available data exchange standards support uniquely identifying students (e.g., student identifiers, basic demographics) across applications and systems. These identifiers and demographics may change over time, and systems processing the data must be able to reconcile these data. Beyond these basic demographics, the client and the service provider should:**

- consider what point-in-time information needs to be retained about the student (e.g., grade level at the time of administration);

- map the program's data requirements to the standard being adopted to determine if and what types of extensions to the standard are required; and

- determine how best to protect student information, if the standard being adopted addresses that need, and if data are required for research.

18.7 Test Identification and Administration Data. The client and the service provider should evaluate how well the available standard supports the data elements required to identify the assessment taken and information about the administration, including but not limited to, assessment and form identifiers (if applicable) and versions, date and time information, as well as when the assessment was started or stopped, duration, testing anomalies (e.g., power failure, fire drill, and proctor comments).

# CHAPTER 19. ASSESSMENT OF SPECIAL POPULATIONS/ACCESSIBILITY FOR ALL LEARNERS

## Introduction

Although most statewide large-scale assessments are, by definition, standardized, they should be designed and administered in such a manner as to be fair and accessible for diverse groups of students with a wide array of needs. Such design will enable valid inferences and appropriate uses of test information. In particular, care should be taken to ensure that students with disabilities, students who are English learners (ELs), and/or ELs with disabilities, have every reasonable opportunity to demonstrate what they know and can do on an assessment. This objective can be accomplished best by following established professional practices, such as universal design in item and test design, and by ensuring that the appropriate accessibility features and accommodations are determined and included in the specifications, pursuant to the contract between the client and the service provider. As guided by the *Standards for Educational and Psychological Testing*, accessibility is a validity and fairness issue, and as such it impacts all students, including those identified as having disabilities and those who are English learners. Decisions about accessibility and accommodations should be based upon individual student needs.

Accessibility topics covered in this chapter present significant considerations for assessment program design (Pre-Chapter State Checklist), program management (Chapter 1), item development (Chapter 2), item banking (Chapter 3), test construction and development (Chapter 4), and test administration (Chapter 9). Interoperability requirements for hardware and software for assistive technology support are discussed in Chapter 15. Data exchange interoperability requirements, including test item accessibility support, are discussed in Chapter 18.

19.1   **A process should be established, implemented, and monitored/ evaluated to ensure that test items, forms, and pools are developed in accordance with the principles of universal design and sound testing practice for both paper-based and technology-based assessments. As part of this process:**

19.1.1   Items should be written to reduce construct irrelevance, to the extent possible (e.g., eliminate unnecessary clutter in graphics, reduce reading load on items containing text-based descriptions). This process should take into account how different students may: (a) recognize and understand information presented in item instructions and content; (b) manipulate, reorganize, modify or combine item information, and strategically apply construct-relevant knowledge and skills; and (c) plan, organize, and construct a response.

19.1.2   Items should be free of language, visuals, or attributes that may offend and/or disadvantage students. The item development process should take into account language which could pose potential challenges or barriers to a student taking an assessment, due to factors such as disability, ethnicity, culture, geographic location, socio-economic condition or status, or gender.

19.1.3   Field tests should include students from special populations (see Chapter 5). To the extent feasible, accessibility options may be explored using cognitive laboratories, small scale pilots, and field testing with populations for which specific accommodations have been targeted.

19.1.4   Empirical analyses should be conducted to provide information regarding how items are functioning for key subgroups (i.e., information that may signal a need to revise or remove items from the eligible pool). If feasible, these analyses should also indicate the use of accessibility features and accommodations by students.

19.1.5   Instructions should be written in language that is easy to understand by all students. When possible, sample items or tasks should be provided for practice prior to the test administration. Such sample items and tasks should include the same set of accessibility features and accommodations that will be available during live testing.

19.1.6    Specifications should be developed and implemented in accordance with the principles of universal design to ensure that items, forms, and item pools are designed to be clear and comprehensible for all students. Such specifications may address the following:

- organization and sequencing of items;

- presentation of items including rules for alternate text (e.g., tagging, audio presentation);

- positioning of items and passages, and/or other stimuli;

- font and point size;

- margins and blank space;

- navigation within and between items;

- ways to indicate answers, such as input modes, response modes, and technology-based response input modes (e.g., mouse, keyboard, touch screen, assistive devices);

- timing requirements, if applicable;

- clarity of graphics and/or item stimuli;

- use of colors and shading (e.g., highlighting); and

- rules for emphasizing words or phrases (e.g. bolding, capitalizing, underlining and italicizing, audio amplification and/or speed).

19.1.7    Items should be reviewed by staff and educators with expertise and experience with students from special populations. The review team should have expertise with assistive technologies and English learner instruction, as needed.

**19.2    Appropriate allowable accommodations, as called for in the written contract between the client and the service provider, shall be offered for students with disabilities, where feasible and appropriate. For ELs with disabilities, sections 19.2 through 19.4 shall apply.**

19.2.1   A list of allowable accommodations should be developed and specified under the terms of the contract and be based on currently available evidence, including information obtained by reviewing relevant individualized education programs (IEPs), 504 plans, and accommodations identified by the client's accommodation policy. The general categories of accommodations may include:

- presentation (e.g., repeated directions, read aloud, large print, magnification, overlays, graphic resolution, braille, labeled tactile graphics with or without text-based descriptions);

- mode (e.g., technology-based instead of paper-based, paper-based instead of technology-based);

- equipment and material (e.g., calculator, amplification equipment, manipulatives);

- response (e.g., mark answers in book, scribe records response, point, speech-to-text);

- setting (e.g., study carrel, separate room, student's home, auditory calming);

- technology accommodations (e.g., refreshable braille, text-to-speech); and

- timing/scheduling (e.g., extended time, frequent breaks).

19.2.2   Allowable accommodations, based on the list developed by the client and the service provider, in conjunction with the individual student's IEP or 504 plan, should be available to students with disabilities. Accessibility tools and accommodations should be consistent, to the extent possible, with those used during instruction and practice. The client and the service provider should collect evidence-based data on effectiveness of allowable accommodations, and must consider the impact on test validity, as well as the feasibility of implementation. The client should develop sound and consistent policies that support inclusion. At a minimum, special population students should have the opportunity to practice with available accessibility tools and accommodations.

19.2.3    Large print, braille and audio test versions, and other materials supporting accessibility should be available for students, where appropriate.

19.2.4    Sign language versions of appropriate materials should be available for students who are hearing impaired; a transcript should be prepared and used by experienced, trained sign language interpreters, or using avatar technology, if appropriate.

19.2.5    Supplemental materials, such as an abacus, braille or large print rulers and protractors, braille paper, and bold line writing paper, need to be planned for and provided, when appropriate for the subject matter being tested.

19.2.6    Assistive technology and/or procedures for oral reading should be available from the client for students who qualify. Training on selection of accessibility tools and accommodations available in a computer testing engine should be provided to district and school personnel. This is important to the extent features are new and/or could help inform student IEPs and 504 plans during configuration and system setup prior to the test administration.

19.2.7    In accordance with state policy, the impact of accommodations, if any, on assessment results should be explained to students and their parents or guardians in advance of testing.

19.2.8    Accommodations should be consistent, to the extent possible, for different modes of test administration or presentation (e.g., large font for technology-based and large print for paper-based assessments).

**19.3    Allowable accommodations, as called for in the contract between the client and the service provider, shall be available for students who are English learners, where feasible and appropriate. For ELs with disabilities, sections 19.2 through 19.4 shall apply.**

19.3.1 A list of allowable linguistic accommodations should be developed and specified under the terms of the contract, designed to match instruction, where appropriate. The general categories of accommodations appropriate for English learners may include:

- presentation (e.g., directions read in English, directions read in native language, linguistically modified test, native language test);

- mode (e.g., technology-based instead of paper-based, paper-based instead of technology-based);

- equipment and material (e.g., bilingual dictionary, glossary, word list, translated text, simplified text, or a graphic representation for a word, phrase, paragraph or answer choice);

- response (e.g., responds in native language, scribe records response);

- setting (e.g., study carrel, small group administration, individual administration); and

- timing/scheduling (e.g., extended time, frequent breaks).

19.3.2 Allowable linguistic accommodations should be offered to English learners based on criteria determined by the client. The client and the service provider should collect evidence of effectiveness of the allowable accommodations, as applicable. The impact on test validity (i.e., transadaptation), and the feasibility of implementation must be considered. The client should develop sound and consistent policies that support these inclusion criteria. At a minimum, English learners should have the opportunity to practice with available accessibility tools and accommodations.

19.3.3    When feasible, and in accordance with state and federal legislation, testing English learners in their native language(s) should be considered. As with all other accommodations for English learners, the impact of transadaptation or parallel development in alternate languages on validity should be considered.

**19.4    The client and the service provider will agree on the development and administration of alternate assessments, such as an Alternate Assessment based on Alternate Achievement Standards (AA-AAS), to serve students with significant cognitive disabilities for whom the general large-scale assessment, even with accommodations, is not appropriate.**

**19.5    Technology-based assessments will be designed to be highly usable by students with a diversity of learning needs and technology experience. Construct-irrelevant variance could be introduced if the testing interface is difficult to use or requires more than basic exposure to computers or assistive technologies.**

19.5.1    Technology-based assessments should adhere to interoperability standards that allow specification of accessibility features and accommodations on a per-item and per-student basis (e.g., Accessible Portable Item Protocol [APIP], see Chapters 3 and 22).

19.5.2    To facilitate familiarity with the technology-based testing interface, students should have access to practice tests or tutorials prior to testing. These practice tests and tutorials should expose students to all item types and interfaces expected to be used in a given assessment.

19.5.3    Assistance with the technology-based interface should be available to students at all times during testing. Such assistance should be easy to locate, accessible, and combine textual, visual, auditory and/or tactual material to support student understanding. Animations of the use of tools and other interactive features may also be helpful.

19.5.4    When designing new item types, simulations, user interfaces, and accommodations, user-centered design practices and a documented set of usability heuristics developed by usability engineers should be used. These heuristics should be appropriate for the student's age and grade placement and should consider the limited time that students may have to learn a new interface. Usability studies should be conducted to determine the effectiveness of the new item types, simulations, user interfaces, and accommodations for special populations.

19.5.5    The service provider responsible for a technology-based assessment delivery platform should perform usability testing for the basic interface (e.g., navigation, electronic tools, answering traditional item types), as well as any novel interfaces introduced. When performing usability testing, the sample users should represent the diversity in age, ability, and computer knowledge that will be found in the actual testing population. Consideration should be given to conducting cognitive laboratories in conjunction with usability studies to understand how students engage with the item type and the cognitive processes they use to answer an item. Follow-up research in the form of quantitative studies may also be desirable.

# CHAPTER 20. ASSESSMENT PROGRAM PROCUREMENT

## Introduction

The client procuring entity will write a solicitation document (e.g., an RFP, Request for Quotation [RFQ], Request for Submission [RFS], Invitation to Bid [ITB], hereafter referred to as an RFP) that contains sufficient information to allow all qualified bidders to understand the scope and specifications of the program being bid. Best practices for preparing and dealing with the procurement process are provided in this chapter. This chapter should be used in conjunction with the Pre-Chapter State Considerations on Assessment Program Design, which covers the overall planning and assessment program design to inform the procurement process.

**20.1 The client should provide a written overview of the program being bid, including the following information:**

- a history of any relevant assessment programs that the entity has implemented;

- a description of the nature and purpose(s) of the present proposed assessment program;

- recent or anticipated changes in policy, procedures, or legislation that will impact contract activities;

- the products and services being solicited, including any requirements for third-party services, such as security, audits, and technology services (e.g., hosting);

- security requirements per state or local guidelines (e.g., proof of insurance, cyber security insurance, content security, access control);

- the beginning and ending dates of the proposed program;

- an explanation of the client's specified legal order of precedence (e.g., Request for Proposal, Question & Answer, Proposal, Oral presentations, Best and Final Offer, Statement of Work);

- the proposal timeline with key procurement dates specified;

- the program timeline with major milestone dates within each school, calendar, or fiscal year, including administration dates of the assessments that the new contractor will be responsible for developing and/or administering during each year;

- the mandatory requirements of a bidding company, including staffing (e.g., technology, psychometric, content, program management expertise), that must be met for the proposal to be judged as responsive to the RFP;

- a transition plan to describe deliverables to be transferred at contract inception and contract closure (e.g., materials, data);

- any content standards requirements (e.g., Common Core State Standards);

- any technological standards required for system components to be interoperable (e.g., hardware, software, networks) and data interoperability (e.g., Schools Interoperability Framework [SIF], Question Test Interoperability [QTI], Accessible Portable Item Protocol [APIP]);

- any requirements related to electronic delivery requirements in terms of computing technology platforms, mobile devices, assistive technologies, technology-based testing strategies (e.g., fixed form, computer adaptive, mixed mode); and

- any special considerations unique to the client, (e.g., procurement laws, regulations, and policies).

**20.2 The client should provide a complete written description of how the proposal should be written, formatted, packaged, and delivered.**

20.2.1 Sections of the RFP intended as background information or general descriptions should be distinguished from sections of the RFP that require responses from the bidder.

20.2.2    If the client intends sections of the RFP for which a response is required copied into the proposal preceding each response, that format should be specified.

20.2.3    If the client requires key questions to be answered by the bidder, those questions should be specified in the RFP.

20.2.4    If number of pages and page layout of the proposal (e.g., margins, line spacing, fonts and type sizes, page numbering, use of hyperlinked cross-references) are important to the client, such requirements should be specified.

20.2.5    Whether the proposal should be bound into single ·binder, or multiple binders, and whether these binders should be included in the same shipping boxes or packaged in different shipping boxes, should be specified.

20.2.6    Delivery date and time, the person to whom the shipping boxes should be addressed, the address where boxes should be shipped, and any other instructions for identifying the boxes, should be specified.

20.2.7    If electronic submission of the proposal is allowed or required, there should be detailed instructions and support for uploading all files.

**20.3    The client should allow bidders to submit questions about the RFP. These questions should enable both RFP authors and bidders to clarify the meaning, intent, and requirements of the RFP.**

20.3.1    Questions should be solicited early in the RFP process and responses to questions should be posted for all bidders, according to the established RFP schedule.

20.3.2    Time should be built into the proposal process to allow for follow-up questions after the first round of questions and answers.

**20.4    Specifications for new assessment components or program designs should be described as completely as possible. Much of this information should come from the client's evaluations and analyses performed using guidance from the State Checklist (see Pre-Chapter).**

20.4.1    Specifications for a new assessment should be compared and contrasted with those for the current assessment, when practical and feasible.

20.4.2    Specifications for a new assessment should include material on how universal design principles are to be implemented into the assessment development process.

20.4.3    If a proposed new assessment builds upon (i.e., is relevant to and must be interoperable with) one that currently exists, test specifications for the existing assessment should be available to all bidders, either within the RFP or by links to a website where the relevant documents exist.

20.4.4    All important specifications should be provided to prospective bidders, including:

- the number of expected students;

- number of concurrent users for technology-based assessments;

- the required number of operational items per content area test, per grade, by reporting category, and, if available, the number of existing useable items available by content area, reporting category, grade level, and item type;

- the number of unique forms per administration per year by mode, including breach forms;

- the item types used within each test;

- specifications and examples of electronic item exchange formats (e.g., XML) to evaluate item portability;

- computing platforms and types of devices that are to be supported;

- specifications for, and examples of, item stimuli (e.g., reading passage, graphs, maps, laboratory setup description, video, or animation) and item sets (i.e., multiple items associated to one or more stimuli);

- procedures for how new items are field tested;

- item pool refresh and item release policy, including the method of publication for technology-enhanced assessment items;

- psychometric approach to item calibration, scaling, and forms equating;

- design of test booklets and answer documents or electronic delivery design, including fixed form (with or without sealed sections), computer adaptive, mixed-mode, etc.;

- security requirements for test materials; and

- scoring requirements for machine scoring, human scoring (e.g., center-based or distributed scoring), artificial intelligence scoring, or a combination.

20.4.5    Specifications and scope for rescores and appeals (e.g., maximum number or percentage) and examples of individual and group score reports.

20.4.6    If the procuring entity desires to have the successful service provider suggest new or specific approaches for any part of the design or implementation of a new assessment, this should be stated.

20.4.7    Item specifications, test specifications, a materials list and specifications, scoring specifications, reporting specifications, and the client's requirements regarding planning, scheduling, and program management, should all be addressed within the RFP in as much detail as possible.

20.4.8     The number of operational items, and anchor or linking items per form, should be provided if the procuring entity has already planned these details.

**20.5     The RFP should specify the numbers of selected-response items, constructed-response items (brief and extended), gridded-response items, essay items, technology-enhanced items, and associated item classifications (e.g., depth of knowledge, taxonomies, linguistic difficulty level) needed for the assessment.**

20.5.1     For reading/language arts items that are passage based, any requirements for authentic, previously-published stimulus passages, or for commissioned, newly authored passages, with percentage breakdown of published versus commissioned, should be stated in the RFP; requirements for number of years of copyright permissions, budget, etc. should also be included.

20.5.2     For mathematics items, any preference for simple computation items that are not embedded in text versus text-based computation items, and for items that require the student to demonstrate different degrees of depth of knowledge, reasoning, and problem-solving, should be stated in the RFP.

20.5.3     For writing, modes of writing expected at each grade (e.g., descriptive, expository, narrative, persuasive) should be specified, and the type of scoring that is required (i.e., holistic, analytic, trait) should also be stated in the RFP. The presence or absence of selected-response items and testing mechanics of writing should be made clear. Examples of previous rubrics for scoring should be provided if new rubrics should be modeled after them.

20.5.4     For science, the RFP should specify the types of stimuli and the types of items that are expected. If any part of the science assessment requires manipulatives or other experimental equipment, they also must be specified.

20.5.5     For all content areas, the RFP should specify requirements for use of electronic stimuli, such as simulations and other multimedia in support of technology-enhanced items.

**20.6 The composition and types of meetings for review committees and other groups should be specified in detail.**

20.6.1 The number and different types of persons (e.g., teachers, administrators, parents, technical experts) who will populate each review committee, and other groups to be included (e.g., district coordinators, technology coordinators, test proctors), should be specified.

20.6.2 The number of meetings for each review committee or group and the duration of each meeting should be specified. If virtual, electronic meetings are desired or allowed, requirements should be stated, such as central location, regional location(s), school districts, all virtual, etc., with the number of computer and telephone connections needed.

20.6.3 The successful service provider's responsibility for paying per diem amounts to each attendee, supplying food and/or refreshments or lodging, or paying honoraria, must be specified.

20.6.4 The number and types of successful service provider staff who will either lead or provide support for each committee or group must be specified.

**20.7 The measurement model for the assessment should be specified in the RFP.**

20.7.1 Special requirements for verifying calibration, scaling, and equating should be specified in detail.

20.7.2 A technical specification should be included to indicate the level of detail that the state requires of a bidder/service provider.

**20.8 Specifications for system and program interoperability should be described in the RFP.**

20.8.1 The client should evaluate interoperability needs prior to or during the RFP writing process. Interoperability considerations may impact the ability of a service provider to address other requirements of an RFP.

20.8.2   Any preexisting interoperability plans, lists of standards used, or requirements from previous program systems, should be identified in the RFP.

20.8.3   Industry standards and specific components required for interoperability between service provider and client systems should be specified.

**20.9   Each bidder will be responsible for producing a work schedule that will result in timely and accurate deliverables. To accomplish this, the RFP must provide a skeleton of the schedule, including consulting services and activities performed by third-party service providers, with critical dates. These include:**

- approximate meeting dates of committee or other groups;

- dates when materials must be delivered to districts or school sites;

- administration dates (or windows) during the year or contract period; and

- dates when student and group score report results need to be delivered to, or electronically posted for, districts and schools.

If penalties or liquidated damages will be assessed for failure to meet the schedule, or if the deliverables do not meet the requirements, penalties or liquidated damage amounts must be clearly communicated and, if possible, specified.

**20.10   The RFP cost proposal will provide a standard document format that all bidders must use to present their costs.**

20.10.1   The RFP authors should consider key information about costs that they need for decision making, and design the cost proposal document accordingly. The client's cost proposal forms should:

- be electronic;

- be formatted as a standardized cost submission spreadsheet;

- be at a level of detail that allows for a comprehensive review of costs (e.g., unit, service, total);

- allow for cost elements that may be subject to adjustments;

- allow for elements that may be purchased individually or on an optional basis;

- specify cost/budget limits if applicable; and

- contain accurate formulas.

20.10.2 If the unit price rather than the total price is required or allowed, there should be an explanation of how prices will be used and over what period of time they are required to be held constant.

20.10.3 The client should specify the key cost drivers (e.g., services for base bid versus options, expected number of students, delivery model, psychometric model), including the minimum and maximum, so that comparable prices will be given by each bidder.

20.10.4 When appropriate, cost proposal forms should allow for fixed and variable unit costing.

20.11 Existing federal and state procurement laws must guide the use of third-party service providers. The RFP should specify any requirements related to responsibility for third-party or subcontracted service providers, including whether specific catagories of third parties must be used (e.g., minority-owned, woman-owned), flow-down contractual responsibilities, approval of third-party service providers prior to use or change, etc.

20.12 The RFP should specify with reasonable detail the ownership of all item content, item data, test results, student data, and related systems developed during the contract period.

20.13 The RFP should specify with reasonable detail the method that the client will use to evaluate the proposals and/or its various components (e.g., technical proposal, management plan, staffing, cost) to arrive at its decision. The RFP must comply with all applicable procurement laws.

20.14 The RFP should specify the process by which bidders can protest the award decision and specify the procedures that will be applicable to any protest.

# CHAPTER 21. TRANSITION FROM ONE SERVICE PROVIDER TO ANOTHER

## Introduction

Continuation of the client's assessment program should be of primary concern for the service providers involved in a contract transition. The transition between service providers should enable the program to continue with little interruption and few disruptions of service to the client, the client's stakeholders, and other persons that the client serves. The previous service provider, the client, and the new service provider must maintain a cooperative and professional relationship to achieve the goal of a smooth and seamless transition. While the new service provider will have its own procedures regarding the management of responsibilities, the first year of a new contract should be structured to minimize procedural changes from the previous service provider, in order to maintain the integrity of the assessment program (e.g., longitudinal data, the consistency of score results). This chapter identifies effective transitional procedures to successfully transfer from one service provider to another.

21.1  **Management of the transition of materials, products, documents, research findings, and other information will be the joint responsibility of the client, the previous service provider, and the new service provider. All materials and information should be provided in an agreed-upon electronic format, when feasible.**

    21.1.1  The parties involved in the transition—the client, the previous service provider, and the new service provider—should each name one person from its staff to serve as the transition point person. The named persons should be responsible for the following:

        • communications within their own organizations and subcontracted organizations, and between the other parties;

        • establishment of a positive, cooperative working relationship during the transition; and

- provision of electronic notification of materials being transferred (including both deliveries and receipts).

**21.2 The client's responsibilities during the transition should include the following:**

21.2.1 Expectations for the previous service provider and the new service provider should be communicated in writing to all persons involved in the transition.

21.2.2 Agreed-upon procedures and protocols should be established and adhered to consistently.

21.2.3 A timeline for deliverables should be maintained with clear deadlines.

21.2.4 Records of paper-based and electronic materials being transferred should be maintained, including:

- a listing of transferable materials, including formats needed by the new service provider;

- written assurance that the sent materials meet the new service provider's needs; and

- electronic record keeping of deliveries sent, received, completed, and still required.

**21.3 Meeting requirements will be coordinated by the parties, including the following:**

21.3.1 Meetings with client staff, the previous service provider, and the new service provider should be scheduled. The persons involved should include a named contact person for each entity and all key staff. Initial meetings should include a meeting of the entire group and smaller meetings organized by function areas. These meetings should produce the following:

- a timeline for transition work;

- a schedule for subsequent meetings;

- establishment of procedures and protocols; and

- a listing of all materials and files being transferred, including file formats and file layouts for data and other electronic documents.

21.3.2   Face-to-face meetings may be conducted at set intervals during the transition, as needed. Meetings may be held for the entire group, including subcontractors, and/or for specific function areas.

21.3.3   Conference calls should be scheduled as needed between periodic face-to-face meetings. The purpose of these calls is to communicate the overall status of the transition, status of deliveries and receipts, and an updated timeline for the transition.

21.3.4   If requested by the client, the new service provider may attend any client-sponsored committee meetings (e.g., fairness/sensitivity, content advisory, test steering committees, technology advisory committees and state TAC meetings) that occur during the transition period.

**21.4**   **Copyright and permissions owned by the previous service provider should be documented and transferred to the new service provider when specified in the contractual agreement with the client and the previous service provider. Copyright and permissions owned jointly by the client and the previous service provider should be transferred to the new service provider. Once discussed and agreed upon, copyright and permissions owned by the client may be transferred to the new service provider, if specified in the contractual agreement with the new service provider. Copyright and permission materials may include test items, test stimuli, reading passages, test forms, and supplemental test materials.**

**21.5**   **Transfer of the paper-based and technology-based item bank contents, item pool, and/or test form information, will be crucial to the maintenance of the assessment program. All item and test information owned by the client must be transferred in an agreed-upon format between service providers. A plan for the security of the transferred materials and data should be developed and implemented. Information that should be transferred includes the following:**

- item specifications, test specifications, blueprints, style guides (for test forms, manuals, and test items), and test booklet layout specifications, including embedded field test items, and a technical description of the rules for item selection (e.g., content constraints, answer key distribution), and the scoring methodology (e.g., method for interim ability estimate, such as maximum likelihood estimate) sufficient to enable replication;

- established timelines for the assessment process, from development to score reporting, for all tests and all administrations;

- book maps and/or print-ready tests and answer key files for the next administration of the assessment, if the previous service provider is required to produce tests for the next administration under the contract agreement;

- digital versions in an agreed upon format (e.g., PDF, XML, HDML, QTI or native file), complete with artwork, test books, items, special versions, and supplemental materials for all subjects and all administrations;

- administration and development histories for all tests and items being transferred;

- identification of technology-based item accommodation specifications; and

- relevant technology-enhanced item or task information and related files.

21.6 Transfer of the client's items for all tests under the new service provider's contract will be a time-consuming process that requires attention to detail. Transfer of items should occur in a controlled, secure environment, using an agreed-upon electronic format, and should cover the following:

- specifications for all types of items;

- all items and associated stimuli and graphics, checklists, and scoring guidelines used in assessments, including those designed as collections of evidence or portfolios;

- alignment information about items, passages, and tasks;

- parameters and attributes of items, stimuli, passages, and tasks;

- item status (e.g., pilot-ready, field-test ready, operational);

- information and all related data about each item, field-test administration, item position in test booklets, and any use in operational forms;

- approved but undeveloped reading passages, stimuli, and graphics, including source file; and

- released items and any items developed but determined unusable.

21.7 **The previous service provider and the client should provide information about special versions of all the assessments being transferred to the new service provider. This information may include the following:**

- specifications for alternative formats (e.g., braille, large print, audio versions delivered in English and other languages, bilingual versions);

- digital and paper copies of each special version;

- prior year's administration production records, including information about numbers ordered and returned for scoring;

- any special instructions for ordering, handling, administration, returning materials, and special security procedures;

- all relevant information regarding accommodations for both paper-based and technology-based assessments;

- description of the process for determining languages other than English to be tested in and the number of special versions; and

- training materials for stakeholders.

21.8 **The previous service provider and the client should provide information about the technology-based assessments and systems requirements. This information may include the following:**

- field technology capacity, including bandwidth and hardware limitations;

- test and item display characteristics; and

- if the assessment uses computer-adaptive presentation, a technical description of the test selection and scoring methodologies sufficient to allow replication.

**21.9** **The previous service provider will provide all contract-based, nonproprietary scoring information to the new service provider to maintain scoring consistency. This part of the transition between service providers may accommodate the exchange of all item-specific scoring materials, so that the new service provider may replicate the scoring procedures of the previous service provider as required by the client. The information transferred should include the following:**

21.9.1   Any information, existing agreements, and specifications that may be necessary for scanning.

21.9.2   The reader training materials with annotations for previous and ongoing administrations, as well as materials for field-test items and operational items, including validation papers, training sets, and score anchor papers.

21.9.3   A list of correct constructed responses for technology-based constructed-response items.

21.9.4   Field test responses and/or range-finding materials for all items and tasks in the item bank not yet administered operationally; if the previous service provider is required to build test forms for the next administration, all anchor papers, scoring materials, and training materials should be included in the materials given to the new service provider.

21.9.5   Details of established processes and procedures, including:

- examples of special codes applied during scoring (e.g., nonscorables) for all items and tests;

- scoring specifications and rules for multiple-choice items, constructed-response items, performance tasks, and/or technology-enhanced items;

- rules for scoring late batches, appeals, and tests returned with responses in languages other than English;

- rules for handling multiple answer documents that must be merged;

- rules for handling duplicate records; and

- scoring procedures, guidelines, and training materials for scoring at remote locations and/or by state groups.

21.10 The new service provider should replicate the scoring of the previous service provider to establish equivalent score results as agreed upon. The replication should include scanning, hand scoring, score compilation, and score conversions. If the scoring process utilized artificial intelligence, a description of the processes (e.g., training and calibration of the AI engine) and algorithms should be provided.

21.11 Score reporting is most visible to the stakeholders, so it is important that there is consistency between the score reports produced by the previous and the new service providers. The transition of score reports may include the transfer, both in paper and digital formats, of the following:

- itemized distribution lists, (parents, teachers, school/district/ state administrative staff,), and mock-ups of all reports, for all tests being transferred;

- interpretive guides for score reports;

- if dynamic interactive reporting was used, a description of the resulting reports;

- report specifications, business rules, decision rules, condition codes, and processing rules for all reports; and

- static and variable score report text.

**21.12** A complete, seamless transfer of data files is essential for archiving student records. Many entities are instituting longitudinal data systems for students where prior administration data are crucial. Data files must be provided in a format agreed upon by both the previous and new service providers.

    21.12.1 The files should include the following:

- the data from prior administrations, including student data files and aggregated data for schools, districts, and states;

- contact information for districts, schools, test coordinators, committee members (e.g., fairness/ sensitivity, content, range finding, technical advisory, test steering), and college experts, if it is part of the contractual agreement;

- building and district ordering histories;

- a sample of the precoded file used to print information on tests, answer documents, or labels; and

- layout specifications for all data files.

    21.12.2 Relevant information for dealing with data and data files may be provided to the new service provider by either the client or the previous service provider. That information should include:

- data review guidelines, including statistical flags and review procedures; and

- business rules and specifications.

**21.13** Records of the process history and technical adequacy of the assessment system maintained by the previous service provider should be transferred to the new service provider. Technical reports should be provided in electronic form, if possible, for all assessments that are being transitioned. The reports being transferred may include:

- previous technical reports;

- standard setting reports;

- alignment reports;

- calibration and equating reports;

- vertical scaling reports;

- research reports providing validity evidence; and

- technical advisory committee records/presentations.

**21.14 Technical specifications for each assessment should include:**

- any data analysis and checks required of the previous service provider by the client;

- rules for combining readers' scores on constructed-response items and other assessment measures; and

- rounding rules for raw scores (if applicable) and for scale scores.

**21.15 Supplemental materials and documents related to the assessment system, including practice tests, whether in electronic or paper formats, must be transferred. The previous service provider should provide the following to the new service provider for each practice test:**

- duplication-ready braille files and large print files;

- extra printed copies of each test, as well as extra copies of the braille and large print versions;

- extra CD, DVD or video copies of tests, delivered in languages other than English and English language versions;

- copies of translation and read-aloud scripts and/or audio files;

- scoring papers, answer keys, and score conversion tables; and

- manuals and support materials needed for each test and special version.

**21.16 Any existing form or letter text that the client has approved for use should be supplied to the new service provider in electronic form. These may include:**

- data forms released between or within educational entities including:

    - between school entities, if appropriate;

    - within the educational hierarchy; and

    - between educational service providers;

- protocols, procedures, policies, and practices;

- answer documents, mock-ups, and specifications; and

- memoranda accompanying reports, shipments, and test materials returned.

21.17 Any existing inventory of test materials paid for by the client and intended to be used by the new service provider must be transferred securely, as appropriate. These materials may include calculators and manipulatives used during the test, test booklets, and pamphlets, flyers, etc., used to inform stakeholders about the tests.

21.18 Any existing materials (e.g., student answer documents) that must be archived per state or federal requirements must be securely transferred, as appropriate.

21.19 If the transition includes the transfer of a support website or portal owned by the client but hosted by the previous service provider, then it must be transferred to the new service provider. If the support website/portal is owned by the previous service provider, but it does not relate to any proprietary products or information, then the previous service provider should transfer it to the new service provider. The format of the electronic transfer should be agreed upon by the previous and new service providers, including the following:

- all resources, text, and items, including supporting materials, art, and domain name, if appropriate, for the website;

- organizational structure of any professional development tools; and

- any templates and HTML text surrounding the templates.

21.20 The change from the previous service provider to the new service provider may occur during a test administration. If so, the following information should be transferred expediently between the two service providers:

- test maps and answer keys;

- operational item pool specifications and scoring rules;

- electronic and paper copies of the tests;

- copyright permissions documentation and contracts;

- order and shipping files, including additional or late orders;

- sample return kit, if appropriate;

- enrollment information used to print answer documents or student labels;

- secure materials files; and

- conversion tables to be used in scoring and/or test equating.

21.21 Transition services should be covered in the scope of the contract, either through the initial RFP (see Chapter 20) or through a change order (see Chapter 1). The client should specify which services are covered.

# CHAPTER 22. SYSTEM AND PROGRAM INTEROPERABILITY

## Introduction

The movement toward the use of technology in assessments has brought the issue of interoperability to the forefront for use in large-scale assessment programs. Simply stated, interoperability allows different technology components to work together. Just as an electrical plug must have a standard, or interoperable, format to ensure that it fits into a variety of outlets, interoperability is necessary in the design of assessment systems in order to ensure that components – whether physical components, or exchangeable data – can successfully "fit" with one another. Interoperability is an evolving topic; while some best practices exist, other procedures and processes are in transition and may change over the next several years.

Interoperability is the ability of two or more systems to seamlessly interface and interconnect with one another, using networks through which end user applications interface, and/or enable different system components to work together, and then enable systems to exchange content and data for a variety of purposes. Conceptually in assessment, interoperability involves components in two different contexts – components of the system itself (e.g., hardware, operating system, and application software) and components of the assessment program (e.g., item content, data, reports) to be exchanged – as defined by the parties using the systems, as well applying to communications networks and data transport protocols.

This chapter describes best practices for improving interoperability and developing more interoperable solutions for use in large-scale assessment programs. Once the client and the service provider evaluate and address program and systems interoperability (see 22.1 through 22.3), they will be better positioned to address content/data interoperability (see 22.4).

In practice, interoperability depends heavily on the use of industry standards agreed upon by the client and the service provider, and employed effectively by all parties, including any third-party vendors. For example, if the service provider uses a customized file format in the assessment program, even if it is a "standard" format, unless all other parties use the same file specifications, the result will be a lack of interoperability in exchanging data within the program. Interoperability may impact customization and innovation, but use of broad "industry standards" implemented by all the program participants often represents the best way to achieve interoperability. However, interoperability is not an all or nothing proposition – it can exist systematically or in an isolated instance where the client and the service provider work together to make determinations about where interoperability will best serve the assessment program.

This process of using "industry standards" will also impact how to achieve interoperability within each Race to the Top Assessment consortium and between them. Since technical standards are dynamic, advances in technology are likely to change the content and scope of specific standards; therefore, the client and the service provider should monitor available standards (and related documentation) to determine which standard(s) will produce the best results in the program. This chapter provides only summary information about existing technical standards; it is expected that existing standards will be updated and new standards will emerge over time, the use of which should become best practice.

**22.1 The client and the service provider will discuss the goals and benefits of interoperability, including the use of available industry technical standards. There are critical junctures where considerations may occur (e.g., program design, preparation of an RFP, negotiating a contract award, during the administration of an existing contract). Among the goals and benefits that may be achieved when all parties are using industry standards to put in place interoperable solutions are:**

22.1.1 More efficient exchange of content, student data, or assessment results between systems or service providers.

22.1.2     More efficient transitions from one service provider's solution (either hardware, software, or both) to another service provider's solution.

22.1.3     Increased ability to divide work between service providers and obtain seamless integration of components (e.g., use of one service provider to develop assessment content, another to deliver and score the assessment, and a third to provide a results reporting solution).

22.1.4     Increased ability and ease for transporting content/data, and solutions used for different purposes (e.g., exchange of released items for use by a district or classroom solution for instructional purposes).

22.1.5     Increased ability to expand assessment solutions/program capabilities with additional services or components (e.g., expanding delivery channels, use of technology-enhanced items, use of online reporting).

22.1.6     Increased automation in distributing assessment results to stakeholders (e.g., delivery of results directly to the local instructional systems).

22.1.7     Increased efficiency in identifying and enrolling/registering students for an assessment, (e.g., coding for accommodations, student information systems).

**22.2    The client and the service provider will discuss and agree upon the use of one or more standards in program design or for subsequent modifications. This analysis includes addressing which standards best meet the goals and objectives and how to deal with any lack of standards in areas and/or any limitations of some standards. The program design should consider that:**

22.2.1     Some of the client's current assessment program solutions may not be based on technology standards, and/or standards for some components or elements of the program may not be widely adopted.

22.2.2     Multiple standards may exist, and, in some cases, may overlap and conflict with one another (i.e., choosing which standard is appropriate for the particular application or process must be considered).

22.2.3    Some standards may not be commonly adopted among all parties participating in the program (i.e., additional devices, processes, applications, or mechanisms may be necessary to achieve interoperability between locations, vendors, or systems).

22.2.4    Some standards may be too new, untried, and/or insufficient, which may require that standards be modified, replaced, or supplemented by another standard, or existing systems must be enhanced or upgraded to meet new or revised standard specifications.

22.2.5    Some standards used in exchanging content/data may not meet all the needs of the client's program design, so that an "extension" may need to be developed to meet or accommodate those needs. However, using an extension may limit the level of interoperability and create solutions between partners that are essentially nonstandard for other stakeholders.

**22.3    The client and the service provider will develop a plan for implementing the use of standardized processes in the assessment system, in order to optimize how hardware, software, and network components interoperate. The plan should address all of the system components, should be organized to meet the interoperability goals and objectives, and should set forth a process for using industry standards to integrate all components of the system.**

22.3.1    The client and the service provider should agree upon what system components can practically be made interoperable and to what extent interoperability is advisable and/or required. These components include:

- hardware (e.g., system servers and devices used in delivering assessments);

- operating system software (e.g., Windows, Unix, IOS, Android) and application software (e.g., student information systems, test delivery systems); and

- networks (e.g., wide-area, local-area, wireless networks, cloud computing).

22.3.2    The client and the service provider should identify the need to utilize existing equipment, software and data systems that differ from recently adopted standards. Where existing components (e.g., legacy hardware or software) and/or systems are not interoperable, the client and the service provider should consider a "migration path" to move towards the use of more, or selected, interoperable standards.

22.3.3    The client and the service provider should discuss and agree on implementing application programming interfaces (APIs) that will be used between appropriate software applications that are part of the assessment program.

22.3.4    The client and the service provider should agree on the best approach for using available technology standards. Considerations include:

- which standards will be adopted;

- how standards are to be adapted or extended; and

- where appropriate, responsible parties to participate in, or monitor, the future development and/or maintenance of the standards selected for use.

**22.4    After the client and the service provider have addressed the areas of systems interoperability (see 22.1 – 22.3), they will be better able to address interoperability of data and content. Among the areas of data/content interoperability that should be addressed are procedures for exchanging:**

- **various data/content related to item development (see Chapter 2);**

- **data related to item banking (see Chapter 3);**

- **data/content related to assessment delivery (see Chapter 15);**

- **student information systems data/content (see Chapter 18);**

- **data/content related to accessibility (see Chapter 19);**

- **scoring (see Chapter 14); and**

- **assessment results (see Chapter 18).**

In evaluating the data interoperability requirements identified above, the client and the service provider should consider one or more existing data standards (see Appendix).

# Appendix to Chapter 22

A number of data/content standards have been developed that could be used by the client and the service provider in evaluating and addressing interoperability issues within a large-scale assessment program, including its component systems. Among those standards are the following:

- Schools Interoperability Framework (SIF) is a series of standards that enable the development and implementation of interoperable software that supports the secure and dynamic exchange of content/data between applications, primarily in the areas of learning, instruction, communication and administration. The SIF Implementation Specification provides an eXtensible Markup Language (XML)-based data format that is independent of any specific operating system or platform, a standard set of data exchange protocols, rules, and interactions (messages) for exchanging data. The data exchange framework employs a "zone integration server" (ZIS) to handle all communications.

- IMS Global, the developer of the Question & Test Interoperability Specification (QTI) and the Accessible Portable Item Protocol (APIP) specifications, provides document-based XML representations for assessment items and tests. APIP, developed by a state-led group funded by a US Department of Education Enhanced Assessment Grant, is an interoperability standard for assessment content using an integrated set of tags, along with descriptions of expected behaviors which can be applied to enable assessment items to be accessible in a variety of formats to meet the needs of individual students (provided in a Personal Needs Profile, PNP).

  Together, QTI and APIP represent a set of open, freely available standards that can be used as a base platform for interoperability, reusability, and customization of digital assessment content that is accessible by all students, collaborative discussion forums, and a diverse set of learning applications.

- Postsecondary Electronic Standards Council (PESC) is an open standards group developing automated electronic data standards to create, store, share, exchange, federate, report, and protect education data through an agnostic, decentralized network (EdUnify), where any user has access to data. Its standards work includes continued development of common data standards, establishment and support of data networks and infrastructure, common authentication and web services protocols, and seamless connections bridging postsecondary education systems to secondary and labor/workforce systems.

- Common Education Data Standards (CEDS) is a set of data standards developed by the National Center for Education Statistics (NCES), which specifies the most commonly used education data elements to support the effective exchange of data within and across states, as student's transition between educational sectors and levels, and for federal reporting. This common vocabulary enables more consistent and comparable data to be used throughout all education levels and sectors to support improved student achievement. Targeted initially at longitudinal data systems, CEDS is expanding to include assessment and instructional improvement strategies at the local level.

- Assessment Interoperability Framework (AIF) is a joint collaboration effort between SIF, IMS and CEDS to untangle the assessment interoperability standards landscape and make specific recommendations about how, when and where to use each of these standards. This effort will address the entire assessment lifecycle including content creation, administration, delivery, scoring, and reporting functionality.

# GLOSSARY

**Accommodation**
A change in the administration of an assessment (including, but not limited to, a change in assessment setting, scheduling, timing, presentation format, response mode, or any combinations of these changes), that does not change the construct intended to be measured by the assessment or the meaning of the resulting scores. An accommodation is used by the client to establish equity and accessibility for all students taking a specific assessment. A change in the administration of an assessment that alters the construct being measured is considered a modification not an accommodation.

**Alignment**
The degree of agreement between the content measured on an assessment and the content standards, frameworks, and benchmarks required in the curriculum (e.g., alignment with the Common Core State Standards and/or the content frameworks developed by a particular state).

**Alternate assessment**
An assessment developed for a specific student population for whom the general assessment, even with accommodations, is not appropriate.

**Alternative form/Alternative format**
A different version or representation of an assessment (e.g., braille, large-print, Spanish) intended to provide appropriate access to the content for special populations.

**Anchor papers**
Collection of papers that demonstrates the full range of score values from sample student responses to a constructed-response item and serves as model responses identified by the client for scoring of the item against the scoring rubric. All actual scored items are to be scored against the expectations and justifications established in the anchor papers.

**Anchor points**
Set points on a scannable page that allow an image to be aligned on the scanner so that a response mark's location can be read in relation to the anchor points to ensure that the mark is captured.

**Anchor item/Linking item**
An item that remains constant between different forms of an assessment across grades or administrations to enable the scores on those assessments to be linked statistically.

## Ancillary materials
Non-secure materials supporting test materials (e.g., manipulatives, packing lists, directions for administration, security checking lists, return packaging lists).

## Answer key/Scoring key/key
Specifications of the correct answer for an objective response test item.

## Appeal
A challenge to the official score derived from an assessment.

## Artificial intelligence (AI) scored responses
Responses scored by software using a calibrated scoring model that is designed to generate scores consistent with those of human scorers.

## Assistive technology
Any software or device, for use by a student with a disability and/or an English learner, that provides the student with enhancements to, or changes methods of interacting with, the technology needed to facilitate participation in an assessment.

## Breach form
A test form prepared and equated to an initial test form that will be held in reserve to replace an initial form that has been compromised.

## Bridging study
See Comparability study.

## Building assessment coordinator
The person responsible for managing the assessment program at an assessment site or school building. This individual, who will work closely with the District Assessment Coordinator, is the single point of contact and/ or authority representing the test administration site.

## Calibration
The process of validation and verification that checks any of the following: a scanner against its original and verified mechanical operation so that all sheets are read consistently; the AI software against its original algorithm so that scoring is consistent; constructed-response score results against anchor papers. Also, the psychometric process of estimating item parameters.

## CAT (Computer adaptive test/testing)
A technology-based assessment in which the next test item or set of items is selected by a computer algorithm, based on the student's performance on items administered earlier in the assessment, and which allows the assessment to be individually tailored.

## CBT (Computer-based test)
A technology-based assessment in which a computer or other computing device is used to deliver a test to the student.

## Chain of custody
An unbroken documented trail of accountability records for tracking secure test materials as they are transferred from one entity to another.

## Cloned item
An item that is generated to appear, function, and perform in a nearly identical fashion to another item (e.g., a two-digit whole number addition item like 12 + 34 = X has many clones: 10 + 25 = Y; 13 + 34 = Z) based on predetermined specifications or templates.

## Cognitive laboratory
Session in which students are administered test items and asked to explain how they arrived at their responses, from which additional evidence about the items, testing tools, and testing systems is gathered through observation or interviews. In general, a cognitive laboratory occurs prior to operational use of the items.

## Collusion
Any planned or coordinated manipulation in standardized testing protocol between two or more individuals (e.g., students, teachers, and/or school administrators).

## Comparability study
A study designed to provide data that may be used to link assessment forms administered under different modes (e.g., paper-based, technology-based) or to link newly developed assessments from a revised set of standards and/or blueprints to previously-used assessment forms under the original standards and/or blueprints.

## Condition code
A label assigned to student results that identifies a specific condition that has been met during the scoring process (e.g., valid score, not attempted, incomplete answer).

## Confidentiality agreement
A legal agreement between two parties identifying how information that must be protected is to be treated when shared between the parties, and what terms of liability will apply to any violation of such confidentiality requirements. This term is often interchangeable with a nondisclosure agreement.

## Constructed-response item/Constructed response
A type of item requiring a student response that is in a written, typed, spoken, or action format (e.g., short answer, essay, research report, oral presentation, demonstration), that may be scored by machine, AI, or human scorer. The terms open-ended and free-response are often used interchangeably with constructed-response.

**Data model**
A specification that defines and documents information in an organized, structured way that allows technical and functional users to communicate with each other and extract meaningful information from data sources (e.g., development of a database with its interfaces to other data sources, the National Education Data Model, found at http://nces.sifinfo.org/datamodel/Information/aboutThe.aspx)

**Decision rules**
Rules and requirements for how any decision in the assessment process will be made.

**Demographic data/Demographics**
Data associated with a student (e.g., last name, first name, birth date, identification numbers, ethnicity, gender, EL status, ESL status, free/reduced lunch status, and any accommodations needed), that can be collected through pre-identification processes or on answer documents, and used for reporting purposes, including the disaggregation of test data by student subgroups.

**DIF (Differential item functioning)**
A statistical property of a test item indicating whether different groups of students who have the same total test score have different average item scores.

**Digital copy/Digital version**
A product (e.g., test materials, score report) provided in a digital or electronic format, rather than on paper. Digital products may be made available directly online or through another medium (e.g., USB disk drive, CD).

**Disaggregated data**
Information that is broken out by various recognized student subgroups (e.g., gender, ethnicity, socio-economic status) or by other category (e.g., grade, content area).

**District assessment coordinator**
The person responsible for managing the assessment program for the LEA or district. This person, the single point of contact and/or authority representing the district in the assessment system, coordinates with the service provider and/or the client regarding aspects of the assessment program, especially test administration within the district.

**Disturbing content**
Content (e.g., statements, drawings) contained within a student's response that may constitute or suggest an immediate or potential threat of harm, violence, abuse, or illegal activity that should be investigated further.

**Dropout ink**
Ink that does not show up on, or "drops out" of, a scanned image, leaving only the marks from the student.

**Duplicate record**
An instance when two identically coded answer documents for the same student are returned to a service provider.

**Dynamic score reporting**
System providing the option to customize or filter score report information by data fields (e.g., demographics, assessment, content area, student, classroom, school, or district).

**Editing process**
After scanning, a process used to ensure that data recorded from an answer document are identical to how a human would record them, which allows humans to check that any blank fields in the data file match up with the answer document.

**Electronic copy or version**
See Digital copy.

**Encrypted data/files**
Data (e.g., student-identifiable data, confidential information) that is encoded so that only a person with a valid decryption key to translate the code can read the data, thereby preventing unauthorized access to secure data while it is being stored or transmitted.

**Enrollment data/information**
The number of students enrolled within a state or LEA, typically provided by class and/or grade, school, and district. Enrollment data are used to calculate quantities of test materials in paper and/or digital formats to be shipped/distributed to each location.

**Equating/Equating item**
The statistical linking of scores on one or more assessments. One method of equating is accomplished by the use of "anchor" or equating items (see Anchor item).

**Erasures**
On a gridded multiple choice answer document, the removal of an answer originally marked. Erasures may result in one or more light marks in addition to one heavily marked answer. In the context of test security, erasures can be evidence of cheating, and often requires the use of forensic investigation of the scores of a classroom or an entire grade to determine if erasures are systematic and who is responsible for erasures.

## Extension
A set of additional characters or instructions in a standard that have been added to the base description to cover a specific application that requires more than the base standard. In the context of software development, an extension is the code added to address a specific application that is not covered by the base program.

## Fairness and sensitivity review
Evaluation of test materials related to accessibility and content appropriateness for all student populations. Assessments should conform to the *Joint Standards*.

## Field test
An administration of field test items prior to their operational use, which generally occurs after a pilot test, using a significantly larger, more representative sample of students than a pilot test.

## Field test item
A test item in a field test (either as part of a stand-alone test or embedded within an operational assessment) used to obtain statistical information about its performance and ability to measure its intended content. Such an item is designed for future test development purposes and does not count toward the student's score.

## Field test sampling
A process for selecting representative students to respond to field tests.

## Flatbed scanner
When answer sheets cannot be scanned on high-speed scanners, images are sometimes captured on desktop image scanners (called flatbed scanners) so that an electronic version is captured.

## Formative assessment
An assessment used during instruction by teachers and students that provides feedback to adjust ongoing teaching and learning to improve students' achievements of intended instructional outcomes.

## Header sheet
A scanning tool used to sort student response data into the correct groupings (e.g., grade, class, and building) to ensure accurate group reports.

## Incomplete mark
On a gridded multiple choice answer document, a marked response that does not fully fill in the bubble and thus will not properly scan.

## Interim/Benchmark assessment
An assessment, typically administered periodically throughout the school year (e.g., every few months), to fulfill one or more of the following functions: predictive (identifying student readiness for success on a later high-stakes test); evaluative (to appraise ongoing educational programs); and/or instructional (to supply teachers with individual student performance data).

## Interpretation guide
Information regarding how to interpret data on a score report.

## Inter-rater/Inter-scorer reliability
An agreement index that measures the consistency between any two or more human scorers who assigned scores on the same constructed response item.

## Item cluster
A group of items measuring common content that may provide a separate score.

## Item development plan
A process for the development of test items, typically including item prototypes, definitions of item development specifications, item review procedures, schedules, quantities, and quality acceptance criteria.

## Item positioning
The location in the assessment in which an item is placed, relative to the beginning of the assessment, beginning of a section (i.e., after a break) or both. Item positioning is of paramount importance when transitioning a test item from field testing to operational testing, because context effects and fatigue due to position may impact performance.

## Item specifications
The defining factors of individual items, typically including content, item types, cognitive complexity, rigor of items, reading passage levels, and the use of graphics, tables, and charts.

## Keying/Cluing to items
Information in one test item may help a student determine the correct answer to one or more other items.

## LAN (Local-area network)
A technology-based (i.e., electronic) linking of two or more computers using a local communications network environment, as compared to a wide-area network (WAN).

**Light mark**
On a gridded multiple-choice answer document, a mark that is too light in intensity to be picked up by a scanner making it impossible, using machine scoring, to determine the student's intent.

**LOFT (Linear-on-the-fly test/testing)**
An item bank-based, technology-based, assessment model, in which each student is given a relatively unique test form compiled at the time of administration, where forms are equivalent in content and preequated to ensure equitable levels of difficulty and fairness for every student.

**Lot sampling**
A procedure in which a sample of test materials (e.g., from one classroom within a school, or one school within a district) is verified against a master list or source.

**Machine scoring**
An automated system for scoring responses to items (e.g., selected response, gridded response, technology enhanced, drag-and-drop, math equation) using a limited answer set.

**Manipulatives**
External material required for a student to answer an assessment item (e.g., ruler, protractor, picture, scratch paper, calculator, formula sheet).

**Meta-data**
A term used to represent all information and attributes associated with a test item other than the item itself (e.g., font size, formatting, statistics, value or weight of the item, correct response key, content standard measured).

**Mixed mode testing**
An assessment system using both paper-based and technology-based assessments.

**Migration path**
A formal plan established to assist a user in moving from an existing system (the legacy system) to a new one. In technology, when a user introduces a new system (e.g., hardware, software, network) but a legacy system is still in use, it is necessary to develop a migration path to enable the legacy system to interoperate, and/or function along with the new system. Over time, this plan will guide the user in replacing its old system with the new one.

## Mock data
Simulated data, in the correct format and value range as real data resulting from an assessment, created as a tool to check operational components of the assessment system.

## Multiple marks
On a gridded multiple choice answer document, an item having two answers marked with similar intensities making it impossible, using machine scoring, to determine the student's intent.

## Multistage/Multilevel adaptive test
An adaptive assessment in which item sets of varying difficulty are administered using either technology-based or paper-based delivery modes. Typically, a set containing items of varying difficulty is first administered to a student, followed by the administration of different sets that may be easier or more difficult, according to how well the student performed on the first set.

## Net-centric
Any computer or other computing device that interfaces with the Internet.

## Nonconforming marks
On a gridded multiple choice answer document, a mark that does not fit within a grid space and requires manual determination of whether the answer may be scored.

## Nondisclosure agreement
See confidentiality agreement.

## Objective item
An item type for which the possible correct responses for the student to select from are limited and predefined. Objective items have an answer key that indicates the correct and incorrect responses. Objective item types include, but are not limited to, single and multiple selection multiple choice, situational judgments, rank order items, and selected situational items.

## On-demand score report
Predefined score report of student performance, generated upon request and delivered electronically.

## Open-ended item
See Constructed-response item.

**Operational item**
A test item used to contribute to a student score.

**Overage requirements**
The number of extra test material sets to be sent to schools and/or districts. Administrators use this overage to provide test materials for students who were not part of the enrollment data compiled prior to test administration.

**Packing list**
A report accompanying a shipment that identifies what and how materials are packaged in one or more boxes.

**Paper-based**
Test materials, including an assessment, delivered in a printed hard copy form, rather than in a digital form.

**Parameter estimates**
Estimates of the statistical values associated with test items, (e.g., difficulty, discrimination).

**Parent/Child items**
A group of related items in which a subset of items is derived from a base or stem item.

**Pilot test**
A stand-alone administration of test items, tools, or a system, to evaluate how particular items function prior to a field test and operational use. The pilot test generally occurs with a sample of students that matches the purpose of the pilot.

**Quartile analysis**
Establishing three points which divide the scores in a distribution into four equal groups, each containing 25% of the data.

**Range finding**
In hand scoring, a process used to identify a range of student responses articulating performance as defined by a scoring rubric.

**Read behind**
A process in which one or more secondary scorers read a student response to help ensure accuracy/reliability of initial assigned score.

**Read-aloud script**
Precise language (e.g., instructions about or for taking a test) that is provided for a test administrator to read to students in its exact format prior to and/or during administration.

**Reliability**
The consistency of scores resulting from an assessment.

**Reporting specification**
Requirements of a report (e.g., what information it will contain, how it should be formatted).

**Response option distribution**
A summary of the number of students selecting each of the response options on a multiple-choice item (e.g., where "A, B, C, etc." are used to label response choices, how many correct answers are "A's", how many "B's" etc. to determine that there is a good distribution of correct responses among the options).

**Root cause analysis**
A problem solving method using a structured approach to identify and evaluate factors to identify sources, consequences, and or appropriate modification of problems or events.

**Scope of Work/Statement of Work (SOW)**
A written agreement identifying the work the service provider will perform.

**Scoring rubric**
An established set of criteria, including rules, principles, keys, and illustrations, used to score a student's performance on an assessment item.

**Secure materials**
Test materials (e.g., an assessment, administration directions, teacher guidelines) that must be protected from release, prior to test administration or because they will be reused in the future, to ensure the integrity of an assessment.

**Security breach**
Any activity that results in an unintended release or disclosure of secure materials that adversely affects the integrity and validity of an assessment.

**Segment**
A specific subset of an assessment typically administered in one sitting.

**SIS (Student Information System)**
The information management system, software, or database containing school and/or district information about students.

**Special population**
A group of students who may require accommodations (e.g., students with disabilities, English-language learners, ELs with disabilities) to the core assessments used by all students.

**Spiral**
A package of test booklets or computer-based assessments in which multiple forms, either paper-based or digital, are arranged such that students in adjacent positions are administered different forms or versions during the testing period.

**Standard setting**
A procedure, based on expert determination, for establishing performance levels (i.e., cut scores) on an assessment.

**Student identifiable information**
According to the Federal Educational Rights and Privacy Act (FERPA) regulations (34 CFR § 99.3), the information that personally identifies a student, including but not limited to:

1. The student's name;

2. The name of the student's parent or other family members;

3. The address of the student or student's family;

4. A personal identifier, such as the student's Social Security Number, student number, or biometric record;

5. Other indirect identifiers, such as the student's date of birth, place of birth, and mother's maiden name;

6. Other information that, alone or in combination, is linked or linkable to a specific student that would allow a reasonable person in the school community, who does not have personal knowledge of the relevant circumstances, to identify the student with reasonable certainty; and/or

7. Information requested by a person who the educational agency or institution reasonably believes knows the identity of the student to whom the education record relates. (For more information, see http://nces.ed.gov/pubs2011/2011602.pdf).

**Student subgroup**
A defined student category (e.g., grouped by gender, race/ethnicity, English language proficiency status, migrant status, special needs status, economically disadvantaged status).

**Style guide**
A specification for how items and forms of an assessment should be constructed.

## Summative assessment
An assessment designed to provide information regarding the level of student, school, or program success at an end point in time. Summative tests are administered after the conclusion of instruction. The results are used to fulfill summative functions, such as to: (1) reach an evaluative judgment about the effectiveness of a recently concluded educational program; (2) arrive at an inference about a student's mastery of the curricular aims sought during an in-class instructional sequence; (3) arrive at a grade; or (4) meet local, state, and federal accountability requirements.

## Technology-based
An assessment in digital form that is delivered through the use of technology, rather than administered on a paper-based form.

## Test blueprint
Coverage of the curriculum frameworks and benchmarks within an assessment, often manifested as a percentage of test items per content standard or benchmark.

## Test deck
A set of answer documents containing all available marks and different intensities, that is scanned to ensure that the scanner is recording answer document marks as expected.

## Test design
Specifications (e.g., assessment type, desired layouts, use of supporting materials) defining the nature of a test.

## Test map
Identification of the order and the manner in which test items will be positioned in a form, whether paper or digital.

## Test specifications
Specific rules and characteristics (e.g., number of items, item formats) that guide the development of the content and format of an assessment, used to indicate what content will be in what proportion.

## Testing environment
The general physical surroundings (e.g., lighting, space, temperature, furniture), standardized so that all students have the same testing experience.

## Testing irregularity
Conduct by either a student or an administrator that is not part of the standardized procedures established for the handling of secure test materials, and/or the established standardized test administration protocols.

**Timing study**
Research (e.g., analyses of field test information, analyses of operational factors such as duration of directions and set up, completion rates, collection of test materials) to ascertain the amount of time needed to administer a testing event.

**Timing tracks**
Boxes along the side of a scannable page to read and verify proper alignment.

**Training set**
A collection of pre-scored constructed-response items used to train human scorers.

**Universal design**
A set of construction principles that seeks to maximize accessibility of an assessment for all students by developing items and content without distractions or irrelevancies.

**User acceptance test**
A preoperational trial of a system (i.e., hardware, software) to ensure that it is working as the client intends.

34499012R00123

Made in the USA
Charleston, SC
10 October 2014